Coping with
Being
Single
Again

Coping with Being Single Again

J. Clark Hensley

BROADMAN PRESS
Nashville, Tennessee

4254–20

ISBN: 0-8054-5420-9

Dewey Decimal Classification: 301.42

Subject headings: SINGLE PEOPLE//WIDOWED PEOPLE//DIVORCED PEOPLE

Library of Congress Catalog Card Number: 78–52623

Printed in the United States of America

To the hundreds of singles again
who, in sharing their pains and pleasures,
have given me an understanding of their
failures, frustrations, fears, and faith
and
to whom it has been my joy to communicate
God's marvelous grace.

Unless otherwise noted, all Scripture quotations are taken from the King James Version of the Bible.

All Scripture quotations marked RSV are taken from the Revised Standard Version of the Bible, copyrighted 1946, 1952, © 1971, 1973.

All Scripture quotations marked NASB are taken from the *New American Standard Bible.* Copyright © The Lockman Foundation, 1960, 1962, 1963, 1971, 1972, 1973, 1975. Used by permission.

All Scripture quotations marked TEV are taken from *The Bible in Today's English Version.* Old Testament: Copyright © American Bible Society 1976. New Testament: Copyright © American Bible Society 1966, 1971, 1976. Used by permission.

PREFACE

I write from compulsion. I am sometimes pleased—but never satisfied. For thirty years I have been at least a semiprofessional counselor and have heard counselees say, "I'd like to have that in writing." This book is a result of such interaction.

A less detailed version of this material is from my former work, *Help for Single Parents and Those Who Love Them.* My experience with hundreds of others since confirms my prior convictions. I have chosen for illustrations the more usual of my listening experiences instead of the extremes.

This is not an attempt to cover all the "fine points" of any given situation; but, hopefully, there will be some help for all who cope with being single again. Those who have not experienced this trauma should gain some insight from this book in order to be helpful to those who are coping.

> I know I cannot share all you feel
> Nor bear with you the burden of your pain;
> I can but offer what my love does give:
> The strength of caring . . .
> This I do in quiet ways
> That down on your lonely path
> You may not walk alone.
>
> *Adapted—Thurman*

CONTENTS

1
Being Single Again

Let me tell you about Buddy, Mary, John, and Sally. If you are single again, one of their stories could be about you. As you would assume, I have not used correct names or mentioned locations in sharing their experiences, feelings, and questions. Since I have counseled with singles again in six national retreat settings, these persons could be anywhere from California to New York. You may hear echoes from your own experience. Later we will deal with many of the questions raised.

Buddy

Buddy, thirty-three, divorced. Middle child. Mother partial to older brother, busy with sister. Father, a hardworking welder. Buddy loved sports. Grades above average, but parents fussed about any low ones. No sex education. Shy. Married Betty—pretty, popular, warm, sensitive, a "toucher," sexually aggressive. Her father, a prosperous farmer,

Soon after marriage, money problems. Too many installments. Two babies. Betty confined to home. Buddy, two years in army, eighteen months in Vietnam. Dated Vietnamese. Came home to job with telephone company. Projected guilt over Vietnam affairs on Betty. Became critical, bossy, and began drinking. Betty nagged. He withdrew. Finally couldn't perform sexually. Rejected Betty's urging him to see a doctor.

Felt he pushed her into an affair with a teacher in school where she was secretary. Each confessed affairs to the other.

11

Stayed together for kids. Betty finally so depressed, felt divorce only way out.

Buddy tried to stay in close touch with boys. He began by saying, "I'm worried about my boys. I hope they become good men, but I've been such a poor example. I wish I could make it up to them."

After Buddy had finished his story, he said, "If I had only known more about how a man should treat a woman! If I'd known how to talk with Betty about things that bugged us! If I had only helped her more around the house! But my dad never did anything like that.

"I still go back to church, but there's no Sunday School class where I seem to fit. Some of my old friends act like they're afraid of me. There's a Parents Without Partners group in the city, but it's too far. My parents think I mistreated Betty and resent the fact that her parents see the children more than they.

"I wish I had been more sensitive to her needs! Suppose she marries again and some other man takes my place as the boys' father. What if I remarry and my boys won't accept my wife? Or she won't accept them? How are we going to educate them with costs so high? Do you suppose they think I deserted them? When should I tell them about sex?

"Was I thinking too much about my own feelings? She was always cutting me down—before her family, too, and even before our friends. She criticized my way of talking, dressing, and everything I did. Sometimes I lashed back. Sometimes I just sulked, watched television, or called one of the fellows and worked up something to do—all the wrong things, I guess.

"Maybe if I had joined her church sooner . . . . Maybe I should have taken her out more, just us two. I really was proud of her, but I guess I didn't show it.

"Well, Doc, I feel better. Do you have any suggestions? Where did I go wrong? Why did this happen to me? Is the Lord punishing me for what I did in Vietnam? Is there any future for me?

"Doc, what about my boys?"

12

There is no doubt that Buddy is concerned about his boys—a concern presently intensified with his feelings of guilt. Buddy asks, "Where did I go wrong?" But he knows. With a backward glance, he is lamenting his wrong turns.

He asks, "Why did this happen to us?" There is really no rational answer except in terms of consequences of the choices we make. Without being a fatalist, one must accept the fact that some of his choices are predetermined by very early environment—such as his lack of sex education or poor sex education that leads to a mishandling of sexuality.

A person in crisis usually is in a state of causative confusion—not understanding what has happened or seeking to deny that it *has* happened. But the big question reflected by Buddy is "What is ahead? Is there any future for me?" This can be answered confidently with a resounding "Yes!"

What are some of the alternatives Buddy faces? He has the choice of working through his grief or wallowing in self-pity and depression. He has the choice of appropriately handling his guilt feelings or permitting these feelings to handicap him in health, job efficiency, and functioning in interpersonal relationships. He must decide whether he will relate to his sons maturely or seek to manipulate them to his self-centered pursuits. In his expressed desire "to make it up to them," he will be tempted to overindulgence, to substitute things for himself, to be the great entertainer at visiting times instead of sharing himself with them in their concerns and interests. In retrospect, looking at the deficiencies he sensed as he grew up, he should methodically determine how these can be avoided with his boys.

Sometimes children are not as upset about divorce as parents may feel. Nine-year-old Pam had this experience: Upon arriving at school the first day, the teacher asked all in the room whose parents were divorced to go to another room for counseling. (How cruel can you get?) One by one they were taken to a counselor. When it was Pam's turn, she was asked, "Do you have any problems?" She replied, "We did, but we divorced him."

13

Buddy may think his children feel as Pam did, but he could be wrong. He might also think that Betty is manipulating the children against him. Even if this were so, it is no excuse for him to retaliate.

So he should get his priorities straight.

1. Buddy should deal with his grief and guilt. God is not punishing him. Our sin punishment was taken by Christ at Calvary. The Scripture "Whom the Lord loveth he chasteneth" (Heb. 12:6) refers to discipline—the learning experiences of hardship, disappointments, and hurts. Indeed, some punishment may come as we bring it on ourselves. But God does not stand over us with a whip, trying to drive us into line. The God of unconditional love would love us through this experience of divorce, nonresident parenting, and personal readjustment. Believe that!

2. Buddy should work on his own maturing processes. The O'Neals, in their popular work *Shifting Gears,* suggest that moving toward creative maturity involved an exercise in self-confidence to know how to adjust to change—to shift gears. Divorce experience will shake one to better self-awareness. As he thus becomes more in touch with his own feelings, he begins to sort out and arrange his value system. He has probably been majoring on minors. Now he can become more flexible and selective.

3. Buddy infers that he may later consider remarriage. So one day he must face the issues of remarriage.

Hopefully, we will help Buddy in these and other ways as he struggles with various readjustments.

Mary

Mary, twenty-five, divorced. Preschool daughter. Pregnant when high school senior, before marriage to Rod. Neglected by father. Too-busy mother. Her parents financed her four years of college. Rod's parents bailed him out of financial difficulties. Made down payment on house when they moved to city. Mary in med school. Rod frequently changed jobs. Mary primarily supported them with financial support grant. Mary attracted to young doctor. Rod accused her of an affair. (He himself had two "flings" in college.) Rod kept buying nonessentials, running up bills. Mary, lonely, tired of heavy responsibilities. Her parents question divorce—never been one in the family. "No scriptural grounds."

Rod feels there is "men's work" and "women's work." Man is boss. They prefer different types of recreation. Mary develops an aversion to Rod—wonders if sex without love is adultery, even in marriage. Rod is vulgar and profane around daughter. Break finally comes. Divorce granted. Mary's depression and loneliness increases some, but she feels relieved at being "out."

Hopes to build career. Receives continued financial support from parents. Sometimes feels guilty for getting pregnant and "having to get married." Feels ashamed of lashing out at her parents when they have demonstrated how much they love her. "How can I make it up to them and still be independent? How can I keep from neglecting my child as my parents neglected me? Where can I find suitable male companionship?"

She feels trapped. She wonders if she will ever really trust another man or at least develop intimacy on the highest level with someone—yet she would like to be in circulation.

"How do I get started? I'm only twenty-five, but that's not like being a teenager."

Mary married Rod and stayed married for the wrong reasons. Her premarital sexual episode was perhaps triggered by adolescent rebellion toward neglectful parents. The parents had always substituted things for themselves and are continuing to "show their love" by financial support in the graduate school. The parents may be doing penance for their sins of omission. Mary may still be accepting help as a means of punishment. But her feeling of guilt now indicates she is accepting their financial and emotional support as an expression of love.

Rod's constant irresponsibility, arrogance, and selfishness has left Mary cold and with a lack of confidence in her ability to relate well to men. Her self-esteem has been punctured. By now she has worked through the initial shock of her grief and has accepted the divorce as inevitable. She still has problems with some resentment and hostility toward Rod. She needs help in forgiving herself for her part in the predicament. At twenty-five, she should look back to sixteen and recognize her growth toward maturity.

Mary will find it difficult to avoid personalizing the stigma since there has never been a divorce in the family. Maybe she will find some help in the suggestions made in chapter 5. She will be tempted to overcompensate with her daughter because she felt neglected as a child. This is sometimes called "smother" love. Her parents may also try to compensate through the granddaughter. It is really difficult to overdo loving; however, if the expression of love continues to be a substitute of material things for sharing of time and self, the child may develop a warped perspective on values.

Mary may face manipulation from the daughter trying to get the parents back together. She may find her daughter suddenly not wanting her to leave.

This reflection of insecurity must not induce guilt. She may say, "I don't like to be away either, but I will be back tonight. We both feel sad when I go to work, but we feel glad when we are together. We have our happy times and our sad times. We may have our angry times. Anger is a feeling that comes out when we want something we can't have then, so . . . ." Mary must let her child know how *she* feels, as well as feeling with the child. She must convey security feelings by assurance of return. She may suggest happy experiences the child may have while she is away and something they may do together upon her return. Care must be exercised at this point to be sure that promises made will be promises kept. Small children have good memories, but they lack understanding of how circumstances may change to upset plans. Too, *being* together should be just as important as *doing* together!

Communication lines (including feelings) must be kept open. She must listen with both mind and heart to the child's interests, changing whims, serious goals, her testing values, fears, joys, and triumphs. By her actions she will say: "You belong. We're together. We share in joy, humor, contentment, in serious and fun moments. Whether present or absent, you can count on me."

Mary is right about being concerned about the prolonged financial dependence upon her parents, a sort of economic adolescence. As long as they offer help without strings attached, however, this should not be a serious problem. As an expression of love, many affluent parents prefer to help now than leave an inheritance later.

Mary can easily find large groups of singles, including formerly marrieds, in the city where she resides. A number of churches have large fellowship groups, Sunday School classes, Saturday night coffees, and other activities for singles. If she lived in a small town or rural area, the problem of accessible congenial singles would be more difficult. She would not be comfortable in a singles bar. She would find acceptance, possibly new friends, and help in adjustment through the local PWP (Parents Without Partners). She might be "turned off" by some of the social activities.

Mary may become further disillusioned about men when she learns that for some a date means "to dinner and to bed." She will develop ways to cope without losing her self-respect as well as her respect for all men, for *all* men are not like that. She may be disturbed about her sexual tensions and consider substituting sex for love. She will have to decide whether she wants one code of conduct for herself and will later insist on a different moral code for her daughter. Hopefully, she will find some guidance in chapter 7.

John

"Death always seemed so far off to me, and I never thought I would be the one left alone. Not that I would wish this on Helen, but women usually live longer than men." Helen, thirty-nine, died of cancer. John, forty-two.

Both John and Helen had solid backgrounds—parents hard-

working, churchgoing people. Both had pleasant childhoods, were good students—education majors, teachers in hometown school. John, now superintendent of schools, church deacon, and Sunday School superintendent. Their son James, excellent student, in college on a scholarship. Daughter Jane still in high school.

James' grief response: "Our family does not have special dibs on life, but we are special to God. He loves us and will see us through." More difficult for Jane: "Why did God allow Mother to die? I don't feel like God is hearing my prayers anymore."

Helen's mother, possessive of Jane. John wants to keep their home intact. Feels it's good for Jane to assume some responsibility. Jane, too old for a sitter, often stays with a favorite teacher in the evenings. John feels "warmly" toward the teacher though she's twenty years younger. Wonders if having such thoughts is being unfaithful to Helen. Has heard the saying: "His wife is not cold in the ground and he's already looking."

He wonders if he will ever find anyone else like Helen and if he will ever be able to really love again. The loneliness is almost unbearable. He fights depression. He is supposed to be strong. James seems to be doing OK, but: "Tell me what to tell Jane."

John is also bothered by the propositions he has received. He was not aware that so many women would actually suggest dates. He feels that is the man's place.

After a while the church people seemed to have pulled away their emotional support. "This is good and bad," he thinks. He wants to know: "How do I put my life back together again?"

John shows the usual signs of working through the grief process with its attendant depression. His busy life saves him from much loneliness, but he is finding that his precious daughter does not suffice for adult companionship. He will have to cope with the grandmother's desire to take over Jane's life. He may have to run some risk of alienating her to an extent. He seems to be handling the grandmother problem well with the teacher-sitter, including the complications of "warm feelings" toward her. He needs to learn how to sort out his feelings—gratitude, common interests, sexual attraction—all these evoke "warm feelings." They could lead to infatuation and eventually to romance, but now these feelings generate guilt instead. They are only signs of a perceptive, compassionate, accepting person who developed a capacity for love. John will find himself vulnerable at this point now.

Partly because of his vulnerability, John is disturbed and a little frightened by the aggressiveness of some women as demonstrated by the telephone calls and other displays of concern. He needs to recognize that, while there are a few vultures among them, most of these women are reaching out in their loneliness, too. Many are old friends. He must exercise care not to destroy their friendliness by rejection, though he does not desire to respond positively to their overtures of companionship. Some of the propositions are out of a sense of frustration, boredom, and a need for being needed by someone.

John's position in the church and community makes him a natural for leadership in a Singles Again group. He should be encouraged to take the initiative in either getting one started or becoming involved in an existing group. He might consider giving up the Sunday School superintendent's position and becoming the teacher of the new Singles Again class. At least he will now be aware of needs he has not before sensed so keenly.

John should be encouraged to continue on his course with Jane. In assuming more responsibility, however, she must not be burdened with so many homemaking details that she will lose the joy of the teen years. She must not feel that she must take her mother's place in companionship with her father, even though they are becoming close friends.

James gives the cue in answering Jane's questions. Romans 8:37–39 helps, but it is hard to accept totally when in grief. John should tell Jane that it is natural for her to question God, though her question "Why?" does not have a rational answer now. She must not feel guilty because of her questions.

There are those who say, "You must never question God!" Well, why not? He is a responsible being. As such, he is accountable. While it seems incredible to many people, there is much scriptural content to lead us to believe that someday he will give an account for what has happened to us. For example: "Now we see through a glass, darkly; but then face to face: now I know in part; but then shall I know even as also I am known" (1 Cor. 13:12).

Why are some spared when others suffer and die? We really don't know. We do know that God has walked through Christ into every human experience, "was in all points tempted like we are" (Heb. 4:15).

What about the hidden scars of Jesus? Rejection, denial, misunderstanding of peers, loved ones thinking him to be insane, criticism, and finally death. He was not given special treatment by the Father. Why should we get off the hook?

John may recognize that these feelings of anger, resentment even toward God—all are a part of Jane's grief. He needs to assure her that he understands her feelings and that God does hear her prayers even when she feels "they are not going higher than the ceiling." His hearing does not depend upon our feeling. She should be told that it is OK to say, "God, I don't feel like talking with you today. Maybe . . . help me to feel better tomorrow."

John should study, understand, and explain to Jane the way grief works. Chapter 3 should help them at this point. This chapter will also help John see how he can put life back together again.

John unconsciously expressed his consideration of remarriage by wondering if he would ever find another like Helen. He can be assured that his ability to love and respond to Helen's love indicates that he has the capacity for loving deeply and intimately. Eventually there will be some good reasons for him to consider remarriage, assuming he finds someone congenial and the relationship ripens into love. At that point he should consider:

1. I am loved and loving again.
2. I do need to be needed.
3. I need the dependability, the routine of a home situation where there is a partner.
4. I need the sense of belonging. I need to be accepted by someone and affirmed often by that person.
5. I do need companionship.
6. He may consider Jane's needing a woman's guidance; but at her age now, this is a very minor consideration. If she were twelve instead of sixteen, then . . . He may have some difficulties with Jane in unexpected possessiveness should he consider remarriage soon.

There are other questions John should ask himself concerning the person he may be considering for marriage:

1. Do I respect her?
2. Do I trust her?
3. Am I comfortable at all times in her presence?
4. Is she of an affectionate disposition?
5. Does she have habits that "blow my mind"?
6. Am I looking for a mother image?
7. Is she kind, gentle, tender, considerate?
8. How congenial are our family backgrounds?
9. What set of values do we hold in common?
10. Does she really turn me on?
11. How does she react to my children?
12. Does she have health habits I consider negative, such as smoking or drinking?
13. Does she have obsessive recreational habits?
14. What of our spiritual concerns and sharing?
15. Do I have a right to remarry?

John, a widower, will not raise this last question, but some divorced persons will. John may recognize some community or family taboos as to the length of a grief period before dating and remarriage. He may decide not to observe such and to accept the attendant criticism. Other considerations of the question "Should the Single Again Remarry?" are discussed in chapter 9.

Sally

Sally, thirty-six, widowed, college educated, attractive, outgoing. Married at twenty-three. Has three children—a boy, nine, and girls, five and eleven. Parents, prosperous. She has been independent, confident. Husband Everett died of a heart attack. He was of quiet turn, reserved, nondemonstrative, but popular because of sports. He was a farmer, a hard worker, but had difficulty keeping up financial standards to which Sally was accustomed. Sally supplemented with music lessons.

"Now here's the hardest part," Sally told the counselor. "Shortly after Judie was born, Mark came back to town. We had been engaged before I met Everett. He called, came out for coffee, and before I knew what was happening, we were having an affair. Mark left town in a few days and Everett never knew. I felt very guilty that I had wanted sex with Mark. So I started being away from home more, leaving Everett to fix his own meals. He never complained while I was working with the church choral group, teaching music, or at club meeting. I was tired at night. He helped with the housework and children. Now he's gone at thirty-seven—so young, and I had always thought he was so strong.

"Now, what am I to do? My parents want to help out, but I don't want that. Should I go back to school? Get another job? Or just live off Social Security and dip into the insurance money until it's gone? Should we move? Should I continue with the church choir? I'm confused."

About six weeks after Everett's death, Sally dreamed of having sex with Mark. This shook her up and made her feel even more guilty. Suddenly she seems a threat to married friends. Even her pastor doesn't come by as he used to. How much should she tell the children about their finances? The boy misses his daddy so much. He needs a man. He is beginning to act out his problems. Once he tried to run away. Doesn't want to play in Little League anymore. He is not doing well in school. Wants to be a football player like his daddy. Eats too much, trying to get big and strong too soon. Has taken Daddy's place at the table. Doesn't want his mother to go out socially. The five-year-old wants to know: "When are we going to get another daddy?"

Sally is mad at God. "Why did he do this to me?" She resents that Everett didn't tell her he was feeling bad. She wishes she had been more responsive to him over the last few years. She is lonely, even with her parents close by and the children with her. She has much adult companionship, but an empty feeling. She doesn't sleep well and eats too much. She might learn to love again—but who would want a woman with three children? So many decisions! So many questions!

Sally, like many others, is in the resentment stage of grief. A sudden death seems to take longer adjustment than a terminal illness. With a terminal illness, the shock aspects of grief usually are worked out before the actual death of the loved one. (Divorce is more like terminal illness than sudden death.) Sally is also projecting some of her guilt upon Everett for not telling her he did not feel well—and upon God for his apparent mistreatment. Most of the time she has had everything her way. Now, here is a frustrating, confusing situation she cannot control.

To add insult to injury, her friends have pulled away and she is not getting the needed emotional support. This usual occurrence is never anticipated. At first everyone is so solicitous. Then they gradually become busy with their own concerns or give attention to other emergencies. There seems to be little or no attempt at follow-up for persons in grief even in some church communities.

The pastor's seeming neglect is sometimes interpreted as rejection. Some pastors are fearful of gossip should visits be made to young widows (or divorcees) as often as conscience might dictate. Others dread the possibility of emotional dependency.

The very real coolness with which Sally is received by some married friends really disturbs her. It is difficult to understand the symbolic threat she seems to be. No wonder she feels confused.

Business decisions plague Sally, and she has difficulty being objective. She needs vocational counseling. She is to be commended for her desire to be independent of her parents. She should plan as carefully as possible for the next fifteen years, assuming she will not marry again. She should not rush into some decision, but should take sufficient time to look at her options.

The children need to be taken into her confidence so she can convey to them security feelings about their financial circumstances. The family unit needs must come first. Wants may have to wait. Needs will vary. There's no such thing as spending the same amount on each child. The children may be led to feel proud of their resourcefulness rather than to indulge in self-pity. How well this is accomplished will depend upon Sally's maturity in handling these matters.

Sally must cope with her son's feeling of taking his father's place. She needs to play "fruit basket turnover" at the table until she gravitates to the head place—or simply takes it. The emotional burden is too heavy for her son. He is fearful that some other man will take his father's place. He must be led to see that no one will ever do that. Sally could say, "Mother is not thinking of remarrying now; but should I ever consider it, Daddy will always be your daddy." She should explain that other men may be much loved and respected, such as granddaddy, uncle, cousin, pastor, Sunday School teacher, coach, scoutmaster—but that his daddy will always have that special place that only daddies can have.

Sally should have some social outlets which her son does not control. However, any man that does come into her life in a significant way will have to win the respect and confidence of the son. This can't be coerced even if she should marry. The new husband would not automatically become the children's daddy no matter how affectionate he may feel toward them. Stepparenting is an earned privilege.

All the children must be encouraged to continue activities with their friends—clubs, sports, and church. All the sports and outdoor activities Everett loved may be highlighted to the son to help him become more balanced in his interests. But Sally needs to spend more time with him, too.

Right now, Sally is torn physically and mentally by what seems to be an impossible job. A source of help for her would be the formation of a family council. Two distinct advantages of its effectiveness are input from the children and a better division of responsibilities.

Sally will make it. With her temperament, she will probably learn to love again. Indeed, she is vulnerable to loving too much too soon. Her feeling that the children will be a barrier to someone's wanting her is misleading. In spite of intense loneliness and longing, she must not get caught on an "emotional rebound." To do so could result in not only the displacement of her energies, but the dissipation of her financial resources. Through patience, consideration of options, and confidence in herself and her children, Sally can do it. Maybe she needs to look in the mirror, point her finger at herself, and say, "Really now—God loves you; and so do *I.*"

I People

Lone . . . ly?
No.
. . . A . . . Lone . . . ly? . . .
No.
. . . Alone . . .
    Always by herself.
    Shouldn't shouldn't she she be be with with some some one one?
    Down the two-laned hallway of my church, up the stairs to the old building, hidden among the younger youth departments, the "I

Room." A familiar place for those who know how to get there . . .
A room for the "I People," not coordinated but a together room.
Unique.

The "I People." Not patterns. Designs.

Jackie. Pretty brownette. Huge blue eyes. Shy but open. Teaches
kindergarten. Church school. Favorite activity is telling Bible stories,
to adults.

Leslie. Plump. Blonde. Wears bright colors. Works for the telephone
company. Can talk nonstop. Good friend to all the quiet, listener
types. Graduated cum laude.

David. Rebel. Non-Christian. Fifth-year philosophy student. Comes
every Sunday. Bought a Bible last week.

Larry. Quiet. Resentful. Can't hold a job. Did a freehand sketch
of Christ that hangs on the wall . . . a Christ with haunting, sorrow-
filled eyes.

The "I People." Single. Alone, but not always lonely. God's children.
Capable. Loving. One people in a two-people world needing only
to be accepted as they are to be complete.[1]

2
You Are Still
a Whole Person

Who are you? Secretary? Teacher? Salesman? Engineer? Do you get your identity by your occupation? Or as a married? "I was the wife/husband of _____." Do you receive your identity from relationships? Identity by position or former position? President of the club? Executive vice-president?

You Are a Person

Who are you? How about identity as a *person?* To *you,* does your name mean a relationship, a position, a vocation—or a person?

You do not have to be married to be a whole person. You have not lost your personhood by the loss of your spouse. You may have lost a part of your identity. People have a way of referring to another as "Mary's husband" or "Buddy's wife." You may have lost some status among your friends because your social situation has suddenly and radically changed; but you are not a half-person because you are single again.

Our essential "beingness" is bound in the nature of God and our creation. "In him we live and move and have our being" (Acts 17:28, RSV). We have fellowship with God and with each other as male and female. Our sexual nature was given to us by God. We do not become male or female by being married. For each of us, it is the image of God in us.

We have gender by creation, but our gender roles are learned rather than inborn. We become masculine and feminine through the learning experiences of life. A baby is named on the basis of gender. Boy or girl clothing is chosen to accent masculine or feminine identity. Our developing roles come by cultural patterns, dependent upon racial or ethnic backgrounds, family traditions, and community customs.

Our self-image begins to be formed as we experience awareness of our needs, our dependencies, and gradually our competency at being self-determining. "I can choose." "I can do it myself." "I am responsible." We sort out our relationships to others and begin to understand ourselves as involved in and apart from these relationships.

Marriage can be the most intimate form of human relatedness. Marriages do not occur between two half-persons seeking to make a whole, but between two whole persons forming a unique unit. This unit is not only sexual but is a totality of life fellowship where two whole persons share an emotional and social relatedness as well as a physical relatedness. Hopefully, this total experience involves a recognition of a spiritual relatedness of the whole being of each.

You May Be Fulfilled as a Single

The question of whether it is the plan of God for all to marry is often asked. Surely 16.5 million single women over twenty-five years of age and a lesser number of single men are not all out of God's will.

Should all widowed persons immediately start seeking another "soul mate"? Society has stereotyped the unmarried as sick, queer, misfit, frigid, homosexual, abnormal, maladjusted, or coming from a broken home or a home where love was not modeled. Or perhaps the girl was raped at an early age or a victim of incest. While some of these situations may have occurred, the stereotypes are seldom accurate. The fact that people choose not to marry at the usual marriageable age, for whatever reason, does not prevent marriage from being a viable choice in the future. Some would prefer to marry, but have not found the one whom they could accept or who would accept them. But where do we get the idea that everyone should marry? Nevertheless, one must admit that in our society, parents rather uniformly think that their children will grow up and marry.

Jesus had more pressures to marry, no doubt, than young people have today. It is rather difficult for us to place ourselves in the cultural setting of New Testament times. Jewish families were patriarchal—that is, the oldest male member of the family was boss. The Jewish young man was expected to marry by age twenty unless he began rabbinical studies. Marriages were arranged by the parents. We must remember, however, that both Mary and Joseph knew Jesus was a special person. We cannot say exactly when he or they became aware of the full significance of his messiahship. However, his peers did not see him in this light. They would expect him him to conform to their traditions. When Jesus passed twenty and did not marry or enter training, they must have raised questions. But Jesus remained single. Yet would you say that Jesus was unfulfilled and his life incomplete?

To paraphrase *All We're Meant to Be:* Each person must come to grips with his own life. Marriage is not what every person needs to live a complete life. The needs are the same, married or single: loving relationships and purposeful living. God has given unique capabilities to each person. Discovering and developing them for God's use is every Christian's task.

You Can Be Creative

The single life can be a creative life. Single persons have the need for sex, touch, affirmation, and sharing as do married persons. Singles again must be alert to find ways to satisfy those needs in an acceptable manner. Coping with these adjustments is the major thrust of this book.

The single person may respond to God's love and grow in Christlikeness. He may recognize that his sexuality is good and God-given. In singleness one can complement or draw strength from one of another sex without physical union. He may know the joys of gender without violating any scriptural injunction as to "sexual sin." The single may accept responsibility for one's place in God's family "to subdue the earth" with the ability that is God-given but individually developed, cultivated, and used. Most important of all, we all may achieve equal person-hood in Christ.

Jesus always responded to singles as whole persons. He made no sexual or social distinctions in his ministry to human need. Martha, Mary, and Lazarus were singles. Mary Magdalene was probably a single again; and the Samaritan woman was definitely a single again, as were the many widows to whom he ministered.

Paul declared that men and women were equal in redemption, as recorded in Galatians 3:23–29. Thus singles and marrieds are equal before the law of God and in the grace of God.

Celebrate Your Humanity

Not all people desire the satisfaction of certain intimacy needs that marriage affords. Many singles prefer not to assume such responsibility for another person. In *The Intimate Marriage,* the Clinebells discuss many dimensions of intimacy such as emotional, intellectual, recreational, creative, work-related, spiritual, crisis-related, communicative, sexual. Most of these can be lived out in relationships as a single. Love as described in 1 Corinthians 13 may be lived out as a single. Grace, appropriating and channeling the love of God, may be operative from one's life toward others. Singles are capable of *agape* love, loving another because of his preciousness, and of *phileo* love, loving on the basis of companionship, as a trusted friend.

Harry Hollis calls attention to how we should respond to our Creator, whether male or female, single or married:

> God calls us to respond to his creative activity with celebration. Do not be ashamed of the fact that you are human! Celebrate your humanity which is a good gift of God! The gone-wrongness in the world is not due to the fact that we are human, but that we do not respond to God's call to be the humans we should be . . . . Not only should we be grateful that we are humans but that we are humans who

are male and female. We are called to celebrate the maleness or femaleness which permeates our human nature . . . In addition to celebration, we can also respond to the Creator with a healthy stewardship of our humanity. Involved in this stewardship is the acceptance of self as a human being and respect for another human beings.[1]

It is my contention that singles and singles again have full personhood to respond to the Creator with such celebration and stewardship.

Who Am I?

I
I am.
I am human.
I am *more than animal.*
I am a little lower than the angels.

I am *capable.*
I am not genius.
I am not able to do all things,
    but
I am able to do some things.
I am confident in my unique gifts.

I am *masterful.*
I am not able to conquer everything.
I am not free from defeat and failure,
    but
I am able to achieve in some areas.
I am sure of some successes.

I am *worthy.*
I am made in His image.
I am flesh and blood, sweat and tears
    but
I am spirit and therefore spiritual.
I am part of His body—the church.

I am part of a plan.
I am wholly His.
I am holy.
I am.
I.[2]

3
Coping with Grief and Guilt

You have suffered loss. Your loss is great and you are grieving, lonely, frustrated, and perhaps feeling somewhat guilty. Death is so final, and no one is ever quite ready for death whether the end is sudden or painfully drawn out.

Grief Is a Common Bond

Divorce, like death, also terminates a relationship that has been significant, meaningful, and perhaps scriptural, and that almost always brings grief. Grief is the common bond of the widowed and the divorced. The widowed do not have the stigma often associated with divorce, but both go through the grief process. It may be brief or prolonged, intense or weak, immediate or delayed, distorted or clean, but grief it is! "We" has become "I." Our roles and relationship identities have changed. A new set of expectations clouds the horizon. Anxiety, insecurity, frustration, dread, and fear, coupled with the sense of loss, overwhelm us.

The broken family is not new, but to each person facing being single again it is a new and traumatic experience. One said, "Single again? I could write a book on that!" Questions frequently asked are: "Where did we make the wrong turn?" "What do I do now?" "Where did I fail?" "Where can I go for help?" "Why did this happen to us?" "I don't know exactly how this came about, but why did it have to happen to me?"

Confusion

Those who counsel with persons either contemplating divorce or in the process of being divorced face individuals in *causative confusion*. "How did we get this way?" "What caused this?" Problems become acutely personal when they center around the lives of two people. Conflicts, personality adjustments, contract violations, and irresponsible conduct, whatever the contributory causes, may become very complicated. When children are a part of the family unit, more confusion results. Often couples stay together for a period of time *for the sake of the children* only to later regret rearing them in the loveless atmosphere of the parents' interpersonal relationships. To maintain the farce of a marriage may be more damaging than a recognition that what is dead should be buried. Much of a child's suffering might have been prevented by an early and wisely handled divorce. But there are always the forces of community, family, church, and friends, as well as an attempt at integrity in keeping a commitment, that often contribute to confusion rather than to a solution of the problem. This is not to condemn or commend divorce, but to suggest that affectional or emotional divorce often comes long before the legal divorce.

Affectional Divorce

What is meant by affectional divorce? A large measure of respect is lost and love flickers and dies. Angie stated this feeling: "He beats me, runs around with other women, gambles, and drinks a lot. I don't trust him or respect him. My love for him is dead, and I doubt if he ever loved me or is capable of loving anyone as he should for marriage."

In all marriages we expect problems and tensions in the adjustment between partners. We expect the children to grow through critical stages with their attendant learning experiences, often causing strain between the parents. Usually this draws both parents and children closer, but others are seriously crippled emotionally by rifts and discords. The suffering of a child in emotional divorce is often greater than in legal divorce. His loyalties are divided. He may fear that he must turn off his love for one parent. He is anxious about the uncertainties. He does not know what he really fears. He senses his parents' feelings and is confused. He worries about their relationship and wonders what will happen to him. In the predivorce period, parents observe these reactions and their own confusion and grief is compounded.

In the high hostility period, one or both parties often go to the minister to get moral sanction or disapproval, if there is need to suffer. They may go to the attorney to get legal advice, to parents to learn how the family will react to the impending situation, and perhaps to a marriage counselor to see if the hostility can be overcome and communication restored. There is grief over failure. There is anxiety over fear of "What is going to happen to me? to us? to the children?"

Separation

During the separation period before divorce, enmity sometimes turns to numbness and indifference as you may try to prepare yourself with a certain amount of callousness for the ordeal of the court and community exposure. Then follows the postdivorce shock and grief, often attended with bitterness. You should remember that the legal divorce is not the disrupter of the marriage; it is disrupted or destroyed long before the divorce court is reached.

Failure Syndrome

The problem of guilt for failure is associated with grief. "What did I do wrong?" "How did I fail?" Facing the stigma of divorce, you may feel guilty or remember things you should have done or things you should never have done. Some recall events before marriage, like a premarital affair, premarital sex with husband or wife, guilt for hostility or rebellion toward parents, guilt over sex (that one is a sexual being, enjoyed sex, or did not enjoy it), guilt or failure with the in-laws. "I never could get his mother to like me." One said, "He seemed to have a personality change about the time we got married. Seemed to revert back to about sixteen when he was twenty-five. He confused me. He appeared to have some feeling of grandeur, but it seemed to me he was very insecure and perhaps afraid, sort of whistling in the dark. He wanted to call all the shots. I wanted him to be happy, but I just couldn't please him."

A part of the failure syndrome is the shattered ego, the loss of self-confidence and sometimes self-respect. A person with whom one has had intimate relationship is suddenly gone. The shattering of ego often leads to irrational behavior, erratic flings, or even to compulsive and hasty remarriage. All are attempts to rediscover oneself, to regain personhood.

Loss of Spouse—Death

The grief experience of one who has lost his spouse in death is somewhat similar to the grief experienced in divorce, yet with different characteristics. Sometimes guilt is associated with death. You may wonder what you could have done to save or prolong the life or wish you had been more attentive, not so preoccupied, busy, or neglectful. You may feel guilty over something that was said or not said. In the event that your marriage was not too happy, you may feel somewhat a sense of relief. It is possible to feel guilty about not feeling sad. Perhaps one has had the subconscious wish or even expressed the desire: "I wish you were dead." "Get lost." "Drop dead." Should the spouse suffer an accident or heart attack, the survivor may have the childish feeling that the wish fathered the deed and feel responsible for the death.

Delayed Grief

Sometimes in the loss of the spouse by death there is delayed grief. One seems to manage very well at the moment and is congratulated by friends and family, but after several weeks or months is found reacting as though the funeral were yesterday. This is not unusual.

Among the signs of delayed grief are:

Depression.—The grieving person may become depressed and lose interest in life.

Self-pity.—Some go through stages of self-reproach, self-pity, or self-punishment.

Apathy.—They complain that no one needs them and cannot be motivated into social interaction.

Overdependency.—They suddenly lose their ability to make life decisions.

Compulsion.—They become overly demanding of themselves, others, or both.

Lack of emotion.—Some develop a state of emotional flatness that may even be reflected in the facial features of the individual.

Processes of Grief

How well do you understand the processes of grief? Separation occurs from infancy to death. How well you were taught as a child to cope with the impact of separation may have some bearing on handling the crisis of separation now. Some separation experiences are natural, such as leaving a child with a baby-sitter, in the church nursery, with grandparents, or a child's going to kindergarten, public school, away to college, then becoming devoted to career or marriage. Such separations as these are temporary; but some, such as divorce or death, are permanent. Permanent moves from one community to another can be traumatic. So separation and the "little griefs" are a part of the natural cycle of life.

How well have you handled the loss of a job? a serious illness? loss by fire or storm? a transfer? military induction? a friend's moving away? a new boss? Was there shock? trauma? grief?

The cycles or stages of grief are given various names by "specialists." These do not always occur in the same order. Usually one suffers the numbing, chilling effects of shock first. In event of death, this may come with the doctor's saying, "It is terminal." In divorce, the shock comes with the recognition that with one or both, love has died. The marriage may have deteriorated by dry rot, withering from within. Some event resulting in loss of respect and trust may have caused sudden death of the marriage.

Denial usually comes next. "It's not so." "I can't believe this has happened." So the bereaved goes to the cemetery to see the grave or says to the "living dead" (in case of divorce), "Tell me it is not so!"

Rejection—that is, feeling rejected. "He died." "I failed." "What more could I have done?" "I wish I had spent more time . . ."

Anger often is a part of grief. "Why me?" "What is God punishing me for?" Mad at God! Angry with the doctor, hospital, parents, friends, third party in a triangle.

Cynicism, suspicion, lack of trust—all are sometimes intermingled with grief. "I can't trust anyone anymore." Some persons in grief seem to have a compulsion to abuse someone. They have been rejected and hurt. They may become especially sensitive about the attitude of others toward their children. And sometimes they may feel slighted by their older children or feel that the children are meddling too much in their personal affairs.

Catharsis may be a part of working out grief. To weep! Bernard of Clairvaux said, "I have sinned in that the well springs must come open, the tears must flow. It is the way God has allowed to wash the soul in the agony of grief."

Some men have been conditioned not to express grief or hurt by tears. "Now, now! Big boys don't cry!" they were told when they fell and were hurt. But big *men* will cry. There is much for big men to cry about or cry over.

"My husband wept when he told me he did not love me anymore and had not loved me for several years."

"I wish I knew my true feelings," he said, weeping. "I don't want to hurt either of them. I love them both."

"Oh, this awful loneliness, this deep depression. I have wept a bucket of tears."

The tears coursed down his cheeks as he said, "Does this mean I will get to see my children only every other weekend?"

"I wish I had her back. I would like to apologize for all the times I hurt her. But dead people have deaf ears."

The catharsis may be in telling the story over and over again, losing a little of the cutting edge each time, thus helping in the healing process.

But after acceptance there comes *pining,* the wishing for the "good things that once were" or for "what it might have been or might be if . . ."

Fear, isolation, loneliness, bewilderment—all are parts of the cycle. (Loneliness will be discussed later.) Depression is an inevitable part of the process, either mild, moderate, or severe, depending upon the combination of present circumstances as well as how well we have been taught to handle the separation experiences in the past. We all have cycles of ups and downs, but the grieving person may suddenly feel low and depressed to the point of despair. Depression may be marked for a time by an extreme "high" and friends may say, "My, he's taking this well." But the mood swings back to low, and it hits hard.

You should remember that the episodes of pining or searching, followed by depression, may recur and usually move in cycles, but with less frequency and intensity of emotional impact as time goes on. So you should not be overwhelmed by a feeling of "here I go again" when something triggers a yearning that is followed by another letdown, blue, or sad feeling. This, too, shall pass! Carol is aware of this:

"I refuse to look at the past and be sad. Today is the most important day of my life and what I do about it today and tomorrow is what counts. I know when I get a little depressed that I will get more depressed if I don't do something about it. I realize that we have to really work at anything we want to succeed at, and I want to succeed at having a good life and being happy and *I am working on it.* Seeing and hearing other depressed people makes me more and more aware that

I do not want to ever get that low. And also it makes me aware that a lot of people aren't working at getting out of the depressed situation. Also, one of the things that motivates me to stay on top of it is the reflection my moods and actions have on my children. Comments from my children at various times have made me know how aware they are of my feelings and actions. Usually, if I am happy, they are happy."

There may be other negative responses to grief. One may be heavy laden with guilt and refuse to admit it or cope with it. You may feel shame from reverting to infantilism or childish patterns of behavior, such as needing someone with you and feeling the desire for physical closeness, to be touched, stroked, or rubbed. Or you may suffer isolation due to withdrawal.

Coping with Guilt

Let's consider the guilt feelings so often expressed: "Why me? I've tried to be good." "God is punishing me." "If I only had . . ." "What's wrong with me?" "I'm the first person in my family to get a divorce." "What have I done to my kids?" "My parents had such a good marriage." "I told her a hundred times I was sorry." "Oh, if I only had her back." "I'm having such mingled feelings. I wished her out of her suffering. Maybe I did something to cause God to take her." "I don't understand these crazy feelings I'm having. I never wanted another man, but now I'm having sexual dreams and my husband has been dead only six weeks. I must be a terrible person."

Tom said, "Actually, I experienced this guilt before the legal divorce, at the time I saw it coming. In fact, I guess I was in the process of realizing a divorce was inevitable unless I planned to live in hell the rest of my life and I suffered mentally and emotionally because of this. My minister assured me that God loved me unconditionally in spite of my 'sin.' As a matter of fact, he pointed out that all of us are sinners and that God forgives us for our various sins when we come to him and ask for this forgiveness. As he said, 'You happened to pick one

39

of the sins that people throw stones at, but is it really any more of a sin than not keeping the sabbath day holy or not honoring your mother and father or coveting what your neighbor has?' This statement alone lifted a very great weight from me."

God Forgets

There is danger in simple answers to complicated issues. One big mistake we humans make is wanting to be like God. We impose the burden of perfection on ourselves and others. We do not have to carry the burden of never failing—of always being right or always knowing the answers. God loves us; we fall short; he forgives. It is that simple. Somebody failed. Maybe we did. But God allows us to live in the present. He takes care of the past. Do you forget sometimes? Then you are in good company. God says he forgets. "For I will forgive their iniquity, and I will remember their sin no more" (Jer. 31:34).

God Forgives

Living under the new way, Christ's way, we can know that our sins, when forgiven, are remembered no more. "For I will be merciful to their unrighteousness, and their sins and their iniquities will I remember no more" (Heb. 8:12). "If we confess our sins, he is faithful and just to forgive us our sins, and to cleanse us from all unrighteousness" (1 John 1:9). When we confess the sins we know, he forgives those sins and those we do not know, too.

God Loves

God loves us unconditionally. Nothing can separate us from his love. "But in all these things we overwhelmingly conquer through Him who loved us. For I am convinced that neither death, nor life, nor angels, nor principalities, nor things present, nor things to come, nor powers, nor height, nor depth, nor any other created thing, shall be able to separate us from the love of God, which is in Christ Jesus our Lord" (Rom. 8:37–39, NASB).

So Forgive Yourself

Your attitude over what has happened to the kids or how family or friends feel about your divorce must be weighed against what was happening to you. As one said, "My husband with his jealous accusations was absolutely destroying me. I just couldn't take it any longer, even with the help of tranquilizers and supportive counseling."

God knows your name. He has your address. He cares about you. He understands your motives. He is aware of your struggles. He knows what has happened. He desires the best for you. He wants you to claim the future. You must forgive yourself as you accept his forgiveness for whatever has been wrong, real or imagined, from the past. To fail to forgive yourself and appropriate the grace of God is to deny the good news of his marvelous love.

Readjustment to Singleness

You then come in your own time and in your own way to adjustment. You have been going through a period of shock and reintegration (picking up the pieces and putting the puzzle of life back together), doing the things you have had to do businesswise, relativewise, and personally. Sooner or later a move is made to a new phase of experience that few take time to analyze. Essentially this is what happens. Loved ones and friends get busy with their own interests, having all good intentions to keep on helping you and standing by. They do not intend to neglect you, but . . . So what do you do? You may sit and pine away in self-pity and think about ungrateful children or fair-weather friends. But what is the mature, loving, sensible way? Begin to remake your life according to your own pattern, remembering that what other people think is best for you may not be best at all and that "the people who matter don't mind and the people who mind don't matter."

How do you begin? Move away emotionally from the family a bit. Begin making a few personal plans that do not involve the family. Visit friends who will not expect a rehash. Go on a retreat. Attend a church camp for a week or even just a day. Go shopping alone, buying some little inexpensive, thoughtful gift for someone else or for yourself. Take a friend to lunch. Take a walk in a park or enjoy a quiet retreat into the woods, by a lake or stream. Vary activities and companions. It is possible for a person to become emotionally tied to you, thinking he is helping you but actually feeding his own neuroticism.

Church? Yes! Later you may volunteer for a leadership post that evokes interest on your part and involves you with people, but don't get overloaded. The same may be said for community activities or those that are child-related and of community nature.

Work? If necessary. But the sale of your time, forty hours per week, to some firm may be either helpful or frustrating just now. It is best, if possible, not to be too overloaded during this period.

Time! Time! The length of the reidentification period varies with the individual. For some it is fairly short, six weeks to six months. Many continue longer because they feel society or relatives expect it. For others, it just takes longer. But eventually *you will* sense wholeness as a person of independence, competence, and assurance, finding the self-satisfactions that are rewarding with contentment and a quiet kind of happiness. *You will* feel a new inner radiance and composure, a new enthusiasm, and fresh daily joy. These processes all come gradually by the moving springs of creativity which Jesus called "the wells of living water springing up from within."

Coping with Certain Hazards

There are some personal and social hazards with which you may have to cope. These are not mentioned in order of importance or in sequence of how they may occur.

Dealing with fantasies. God has given us two of our best blessings in memory and imagination. Because of these two faculties of the mind, we are able to fantasize—imagine our-

42

selves in a given situation, wondering what it would be like. Through imagination and memory we experience some of the actual feelings of the situation. We have the ability to project ourselves into other situations. Those who read or watch a movie identify with the characters and thus feel with them. This is not bad. Neither is it bad to have some fantasy experiences that produce sensations needed to maintain the feeling of being alive.

Friendship with members of the opposite sex. Object: companionship. This is difficult because it is hard to know whom we can trust. With whom are we companionable? A widow, widower, or divorcee is fair game for a jealous mate, but there are those friends with whom we can relate on this basis. And there is definitely a human need to do so. But hazards exist. It must be admitted also that some seek friendship only for coital relationships.

Emotional exploitation. All have emotional needs—for warmth, appreciation for what we are and think, consideration of our person and our ideas. These needs may be exploited, not with helpful intent but for ego purposes or pleasure of others. You must protect yourself by being aware that these persons are constantly looking for an opportunity to "stalk their prey." They are not always of the opposite sex. When aware that such is happening, drop them!

Emotional rebounds. As you move through the period of readjustment and the emotional pendulum swings back toward equilibrium, you may be in danger of reaching out to anyone who comes along and is available. During this period when you are most vulnerable, you may be less capable of making value judgments concerning the character of, or congeniality with, another person and of separating romance from love. However, romance must be kept in life. By this we refer to love for beauty, art, of expressing appreciation and gratitude, love for the poetic, some appreciation for music, relating to nature—sun, stars, flowers, trees, wind, rain, a storm, the softness of a voice, the breath of a whisper, or the warmth of a touch.

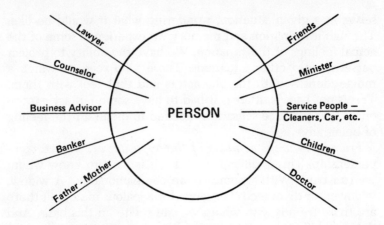

Need to spread dependencies. Before, you have been primarily dependent upon one person. Now this must be diffused. You do not trade one dependency for another, but you become more independent and self-sufficient in a sense. Perhaps self-directing is a better phrase since no one is self-sufficient.

Your dependencies are spread to "significant others," but you are not dependent upon any one of them. You are keeping your identity and direction as a person and not leaning upon them in a self-destructive manner. You transfer your dependencies and diffuse them rather than clinging to one person. In the process of diffusion one learns to be self-reliant, self-sufficient, and self-directing.

All of this sounds rather methodical and structured, but hazards are not faced by a structured method. You must learn, however, to cope by a structured approach in order to avoid them completely or keep from being surprised and "bowled over."

Dawn Encounter

Good morning, God.
The first red glow of your morning sun is slipping over the hills.

Only one morning star remains and the city is beginning to awaken and turn off its night lights.

A gentle wind is bringing the smell of the pine trees closer.

The heavy dew has refreshed the grass and the air.

It feels good to be out here with you, Lord.

It should be a great day.

I want to be alive in it . . . completely, totally alive, with nothing crushing me down or holding me back.

Take away the guilt of yesterday's mistakes, Lord.

Help me to put them as far out of my mind as you promised to put them out of yours, trusting you to blot them out so that they may never separate us again.

Don't let me clutter up today, Lord, with a lot of burdens I should leave here at your feet.

Help me to stop struggling over problems I have already committed to you.

Don't let me get hung up on the uncertainties of tomorrow.

Free me, Lord, to love and be loved.

Free me to experience, to absorb, to explore, to grow, to appropriate the richness of the life you offer.

Let my soul match the freshness of this new day.

It feels good to be out here with you, Lord.

It should be a great day.[1]

4
Coping with
Loneliness and Boredom

The first divorce was not between man and woman
   but between man and God.
And the Garden must have been lonely for God
   after Adam and Eve were gone.[1]

Your wife has been dead a month and as you look at yourself in the mirror you say, "Oh, God, what am I going to do?"

People see you and ask, "How are you getting along?" You answer, "Fine." But you are really having a very hard time with loneliness—aching, gnawing loneliness.

"I would like to say that besides the emotions of *happy* and *sad* there is *emptiness*. I have learned that unless I have someone of the opposite sex to care about, and who cares about me, I am empty. I think that most divorced or widowed people feel this way. It is beyond lonely. I'm a Christian. I pray a lot. I read my Bible, and I truly feel that the Lord is with me always. But this does not quite fill the emptiness."

Kathy, who has experienced both losses, states that divorce is more lonely than death. She says: "I think I was more lonely after my divorce than after my second husband died. People rally to you in death, but you do not get much support in divorce."

This cry is echoed in the form of a prayer:

I write this to you, God, with the hope that you will understand.
I feel lost, separated, and totally alone, and yet, there are many close by. I wonder where I can find the happiness and peace of mind I so desperately want. I need the closeness and total caring of another

46

being, and yet the ones for whom I care are incapable of caring for anyone but themselves.

I have the children, and that should be sufficient, but after they are in bed, the loneliness and need are much more than I can take.

Please help me, God, to find the peace I so desperately need and the wisdom to know how to handle it when I find it.

God, help this feeling of emptiness to be filled with other things which are of value to both myself and my children.

Help me not to grab for just anything to fill the loneliness and help me to realize my importance to myself, my self-confidence in myself, as I seem to have lost them along the way.

Guide me with people as I seem to reach for the ones who can hurt me the most. When I reach for those whom I allow to hurt me, hold me tightly and help me to pull away from them and closer to things which are truly important.

Teach me that to be alone is not the worst thing in the world. Help me realize this, as this is my biggest problem.

Loneliness makes me frightened of the future, regretful of the past, and dissatisfied with the present—help me to fill this void.

Help me to erase my desire to seek revenge on those who have hurt me, and replace it with a forgiving spirit, realizing I may hurt others, and I myself need forgiveness.

And, dear Lord, help me to learn to trust again. Amen.[2]

Living with Loneliness

This intense loneliness one feels in a loss experience cannot be ignored. The world of the formerly married is rather like a state of limbo, being located on the edge of society. One feels like an odd-ball, a tagalong, and feels left out of things. Social groups are organized for twosomes. Society does not make place for the single person, the formerly married. Women who are divorced or widowed suddenly find themselves a "target for the night." The price of a dinner and movie may turn out to be a proposed trip to a man's apartment (or hers) and to bed. Not all men divorced or widowed are "on the prowl." Many are deterred by conscience, others by circumstances of family, custom, or religious commitment.

Men are often shocked to learn that some women are ready to pounce upon them in their loneliness and aggressively seek their companionship by telephone, direct solicitation of dates,

and more subtle ways. To succumb to these overtures by following the path of least resistance does not fill the aching void,
but usually leads to more emptiness and deeper loneliness.

Another more positive response is reflected in one of the
poems of Peggy S. Buck, a teacher in Fort Bragg, North
Carolina.

> Lord,
> if I only learn
> one thing
> from pain,
> I ask for this—
> Let me break no branches,
> destroy no flowers
> as I pass.
> Teach me gentleness,
> compassion,
> And all the tears
> that I have cried
> will be
> acceptable, justified.[3]

It helps first to realize that most people are lonely much
of the time. Even the mature and happily married have these
moments, days, or even weeks. But you think, *Yes, but they
have the hope of their loved one returning to share, and this
buoys them up.* True, but it does not always alleviate the immediate throes of isolation.

"Well, I married for love and security," Patsy laments, "but
he wanted another mother and housekeeper with sex attached.
Saturday was for hunting and fishing or playing basketball. Sunday—church, maybe. Me? Oh, I was supposed to sit around
and wait for him or wait *on* him—fix his meals, do his laundry,
be available when he needed or wanted me, no matter about
my wishes or needs."

Meaningful Relationships

The cure for loneliness is meaningful relationships with others. When a man offers a woman only a sexual relationship,

this cannot have much meaning. When one offers another only an exploitative relationship, this is less than meaningful. In the diffusion of dependencies, as stated before, one must draw on several sources without "overdrawing the account" on anyone. Two or three intimate friends, perhaps five at the most, is all the luxury one can afford. If they can all be old friends, the better. Sometimes one is shocked to realize that the friendship he has experienced with another was based on a twosome relationship and now the person is either less understanding than before or seems reluctant to continue the friendship. Unfortunately, there is often room for misunderstanding or jealousy on the part of the friend's mate. The other feels deprived of the attention or time given. Fear of jealousy haunts the single person. So the single's loneliness is accentuated by the change in relationship with former friends.

Take time to find the type of people you like and would enjoy as friends, those to whom you can give and from whom you can receive. As you go to musical concerts, theaters, clubs, or church meetings, you will meet many new people. Learn to form suspended judgments. Give potential friends a chance to get acquainted with you. Attend events or form associations only with enjoyable groups. Do not waste your time in an endless round of meaningless activities.

There are many other coping devices for loneliness. Use the telephone to call a friend or relative, expressing interest in him or appreciation for him. Be careful not to impose on his time by lengthy conversations. By using telephone manners, your calls will be welcomed and not regarded as an imposition. Entertain in a relaxing manner. Include your child or children in some of this.

Be careful not to throw away your privacy and take great care not to overtax your energy in church or community work, thinking it can dispel loneliness. There should be other compensations in such activity, but this is not one of them.

Study to improve your relationship with your child or children so it will be mutually more enjoyable. However, as stated before, this must not substitute for adult companionship.

You Do Need a Friend

The close friend or confidant may be the person used to test your attitude to see if you are ready to relate socially as a single again. Everyone needs to share experiences with someone else. Shortly after one man became a widower, he was given an appreciation dinner by his firm. His response was, "All of this is wonderful, but I do not have anyone to tell my happiness to anymore."

One's own inner security may be fortified by a restudy of himself during this period of adjustment. It may sound rather ridiculous, but in the case of a marriage failure, it is imperative to make a new study on the question of "getting ready for marriage" such as is suggested by David R. Mace in his book by that title. Granted that the situation would be considerably different in a second marriage, a review of your experience with the former spouse may move you from scapegoating to discovering some of your own hang-ups. No doubt you should decide to act differently if you consider remarriage.

You May Not Want to Date

Obviously there are some people who do not care to date or relate to a person of the opposite sex on a personal basis. Some widows and widowers fall in this category. But many have at least a yearning of hostility and anger that one still carries for his former spouse. These may cause him to feel, "I don't want to be hurt again." Consequently, he will avoid any such involvement.

Some who have lost their spouse by death are so loyal to this first love that they find it difficult to entertain the thought of dating. Many who consider the thought dismiss it immediately for various reasons. Others wait until their children are grown before they give any consideration to the idea of companionship with someone of the opposite sex or remarriage. The idea of relating and dating may be delayed because the single life seems more agreeable than marriage and because intimacy with another person is not desired.

Friends and relatives may suggest that you date long before you feel you should. No matter what others think, you should not date until you personally feel like it. Then don't be afraid to let others know of your interest in dating. Sometimes asking for a date is a big hurdle for the male due to the fear of being rejected. Another fear may be alleviated if one of the ex-spouse's family suggests that it might be wise if he considers dating, especially if the suggestion is for his sake and not because "the children need a mother."

What about the children? They should not be allowed to control the social life of the parent, and this includes dating. The noncustodial parent, usually the father, may date without being seen by the children, so they are not wondering and asking questions about it. But if the mother is living with her children, she has more difficulty. If, during the period of readjustment, she has entertained friends that include both sexes, her children will not be too curious or perhaps anxious as she receives male callers.

The purpose of dating may involve either companionship, emotional involvement, or the selection of a mate. The person who has been married usually does not go into the dating and relating relationship with any thought except companionship, only to find that emotional involvement and the mate selection come later. After deliberation, some desire to marry again.

Many women express the need to "feel like a woman," to feel attractive to the opposite sex. This does not mean they expect sex from the men they date but feel the need to be accepted for themselves as persons. Betty badly needs to restore self-esteem. "I have been told by my ex so often how unattractive I am and how incapable I am of doing anything right that he has made me believe it. I can't imagine any man finding me desirable in any way. But I have decided I'm going to join a church group and Parent Without Partners group and see what happens. Maybe I'll be reassured again and regain my confidence. I'll have difficulty responding to friendships, but I'm going to make myself do it if anyone notices I'm around."

Getting Back into Circulation

A very attractive single again exclaims: "I get so lonely at night. There's not much to do. I used to sew a lot, but I'm tired of that. Mostly old people live in my apartment complex. I've seen a few younger guys out around the pool, but when one takes a second look at me I want to run. I hate to get into a bathing suit or shorts. My skin is so white and creamy looking. I wish I had a tan. Maybe I'd like myself better. How do you have the nerve to make yourself available—even for conversation?"

A big question: How *do* you get back into circulation and find people to whom you can relate? One reported that she has received all these suggestions: join the country club, take up a hobby, lose weight, join another church, go on a trip. There are many ways. Married friends are anxious to make introductions, or unmarried friends may help. Others find possibilities in their jobs, professional circles, churches, and through community events or social clubs. Parents Without Partners and such organizations provide opportunities to meet eligibles. Vacation time, resorts, and so forth offer other opportunities. We would hardly recommend the "pickup" or the "open parties" or certain friendship clubs, mail order lists, or computer dating.

A mature adult does not have to be as subtle as a teenager. Both men and women can be more frank. The rules of courtesy in dating, however, ought to be as applicable. For instance, the gentleman asks the lady to a specific event at a specific time instead of asking, "What are you going to be doing Saturday night?" Obvious rules of courtesy would include calling for the date at her door or going in to meet the family if it seems the best course of action. One may reasonably ask, "What is wrong with meeting at the church or some other convenient place if each has transportation and time or convenience is a factor?" Nothing!

As for affection or intimacy, this may depend upon how well

acquainted the couple is and if the relationship is a warm one. Intimacy here does not refer to sexual intimacy.

To protect her self-respect, arrangements for her children should be the woman's responsibility, at least until there is some frequency pattern established or the gentleman knows that she simply cannot afford the cost of a baby-sitter. A man should not splurge or overspend on flowers, gifts, or entertainment in order to impress. A phony will soon be found out.

How do you act on a date? "Do to others as you would have them do to you" in a very natural sort of way. Act with openness, courtesy, and respect.

A woman is not necessarily considered too aggressive if she develops some subtle method of letting a man know that she is interested in him. She may need his advice or help. She may have some tickets to an event and need an escort. There may be places she cannot go by herself, so he is asked to go along. She may need a ride. She may invite him in for coffee. These are suggestions women may use in taking the initiative to say, "I would enjoy your companionship." "I am interested in you." "I have confidence in you." "I would like to know you better."

The Children and Your Date

For some, there are still the children. Children should not be expected to bear the emotional burden of questions pertaining to dating and remarriage. Many want their parents to marry again, while most want them to remarry each other, frequently asking if they are going to do so. This question may reflect insecurity. On the other hand, when the mother or father starts dating, children can become jealous and overanxious, wondering about a remarriage. Some even ask their mother's date if he is going to be their new daddy. Women often prefer not to introduce their children to every man they date, but only to those they are interested in.

The children should be reminded that part of their parents' lives is private and even though they may or may not want them to marry again, there is nothing to fear. These children need to be assured over and over that the parents' love for them will not change and can include another person without taking any love away from them. Counsel may be needed as to the advisability of children observing affectionate expressions between a couple not ready to announce their engagement or plans for marriage.

What Can I Do If I Don't Date?

Those who are not interested in relating or mating may well be asking: "Well, what's in all of this for me? Does it mean that I will never be able to enjoy the companionship of the opposite sex? Does it mean that I will have to confine my social experiences to groups and be the sore thumb at a party or social event? Does it mean that I shall continue to be out of place at church, community events, and other activities?"

Perhaps the answer to these questions depends upon the individual. If you make yourself attractive in personality, congenial in manner, and cooperative in social relationships, your presence may well be desired at most social gatherings whether or not you have a companion. A woman must be careful not to be a threat to other women, especially with reference to their husbands. Yet if she is quite natural with everyone in the group, treating male and female alike, she ought not to pose a threat. There will be a few jealous souls in almost any group, and she may learn to avoid them. A man may be accepted for who he is as a person and find his companionship enjoyed by others in the group.

Most communities have some singles groups. Larger communities have Parents Without Partners, which is perhaps the best known of the organizations. There are usually four groups of singles in any given community: (1) those who have never married and are in the younger group, looking toward marriage, (2) those who have never married and are in an older age group, who have perhaps decided against marriage or who cannot marry, (3) those in the younger group who have lost their spouse by death or divorce, and (4) those in the older group who have lost their spouse by death or divorce. The nature of circumstances concerning each of these groups causes them to have different interests, and they sometimes find it hard to mix in a singles group. For the older group, there are clubs that serve a very useful purpose as a fellowship and service outlet for those beyond retirement.

Many communities have adult programs in the YMCA and YWCA. Adult education classes are beginning to be quite common. There are other groups, such as country clubs, bowling leagues, ball teams, fraternities, sororities, professional organizations, lodges, hobby clubs, and so forth. Many singles again desire something that has educational or inspirational value. Others prefer only recreational activities and relaxation. Sometimes an organization starts from one point of view and after several months takes on a new trend or dimension, depending upon the desires and needs of the membership. Some church organizations sponsor groups to which singles may belong.

Thus individuals who are not interested in actual dating may find participation in group activities and organizations without being vulnerable to what they may feel to be the hazards of dating. Usually you can choose a group that will fit your time schedule and financial resources. If you begin to date, you may find considerable support and help from this group. Those familiar with various singles clubs know that some dating members continue some involvement with the club. Some who remarry find a continued interest and supportive relationship with friends in the singles group.

Boredom

Boredom is often a part of loneliness. What do you do when you don't have anything to do? Among the things that can make one bored are: (1) an unchallenging job, (2) unfulfilling friends, (3) disenchanting living accommodations, (4) lack of opposite sex relationships or adult relationships, (5) not enough to do, and (6) too much self-reliance.

These comments may help to illustrate previously mentioned situations:

"My job is just the same old six and seven. I never get to see people. All I ever see is the typewriter. I deal with the same old figures and same old forms week in and week out."

"My friends never challenge me. You would think they had never been away from home. Their interests lie entirely in weather, sports, what they're going to eat, or what they've had to eat."

"I live in an apartment complex with very few people my age around. It seems most of the men are rejects like me. Where do you go to find someone you can trust to be your friend or even a companion?"

"I get so tired of talking with women, I don't know what to do." (A woman's comment.)

"I get so tired of talking to children and not having any adult conversation that I could just climb the wall."

"My job is not too exacting physically, so I have a lot of energy left over in the evening. But I don't have anywhere to spend it or anyone to spend it with."

"I guess I'm too satisfied with being on my own. I prefer not to have anyone around much. I think I'm perfectly capable of handling my own affairs."

We need to differentiate between privacy, loneliness, and solitude. Solitude may be a gift that enables a person to enjoy the pleasures of his own special world. Privacy means just being alone, which may mean alone in loneliness or in solitude. We all have the need for privacy and should expect our children to respect our privacy as we respect theirs. We need time for our own private thoughts; and this sometimes means going to our room and closing the door. We need to learn to live with ourselves. We need to learn how to explore our own private resources and renew the vital elements of our own personality and character that nourishes us for a relationship with others. Enjoying ourselves alone may be a prerequisite for genuinely enjoying others.

Sometimes when we are single we fear being alone, especially if we happen to be in ill health. We are afraid of being sick with no one else there.

Ann Alexander, a single again, in leading a retreat seminar, made some positive suggestions for coping with boredom and loneliness:

1. Self-improvement may be helpful. This might involve going on a diet, taking up good exercise habits, and seeking to improve or change our appearance. It might involve breaking bad habits and especially watching our general health care.

2. As a part of self-improvement, we could develop new interests, learn a new language, develop some new skills, study some new subjects, broaden our reading habits, consider travels in our annual schedules, or take up handcrafts, some mechanical hobby, or gourmet cooking.

3. It may be good to remember and reactivate an old interest or to recycle something good that we have let go—especially activities involving people.

4. Maybe we should invite some new people into our lives and be open to new people, new ideas, new places, and new experiences. It would be good for us to face the fact that "Maybe life was not boring; I was" or "Life is not boring; I am."

5. We could well become involved in working with our local legislators to get some better laws dealing with family, child care, and related matters that involve single people.

6. We can express our caring for others. In almost any community, there is a rest home for the convalescing or aging. A regular routine for visiting may work wonders for us. Look around. Visit some shut-in who lives within your immediate community. Is there someone in your area who needs a baby-sitter now and then? You could offer your services to give the mother or the father a night out or morning off. Most communities have need for hospital volunteer workers. Some of these activities can be done in the evening. In our city the CONTACT Teleministry, a crisis intervention program, always has need for telephone workers; and a wonderful training program is suggested for those who can help.

7. Perhaps you should say, "I will not wait to share myself with the world; I will do it today. It does need me. I will learn

better how to hang loose in this uptight world. I believe I will become a stronger person, a different person, a more involved person, and a less lonely and bored person if I do this."

Sharla has found this answer: "To begin with, I stay very busy, not doing busywork but doing things which I enjoy—things that are (1) meaningful to me, and/or (2) challenging to me, and/or (3) meaningful to others (a contribution to others of some kind), and/or (4) meaningful to my family and a means of building my relationships with my children.

"When I try to summarize these things, I realize they all involve a sharing of myself and my abilities, whatever they may be, whether they are sharing with my family, my friends, people in need, or God. Along this same line, I believe that the abilities I am speaking of are not special talents, but include such things as the ability to laugh at oneself, the ability to be genuine and real with oneself and others, and the ability to just be there when someone needs you. There is no loneliness or boredom when you can share this kind of thing with those around you.

"More practically, I should add that the role of my newly acquired single friends has been important to overcoming loneliness and boredom. If I ever find myself with nothing to do—which is almost a laugh—or, and more likely, with the need for a 'change of channels' (the need to get out and do something different), there is always someone around who welcomes this idea. I have always been able to find someone to share my change of channels with. I really do wish more people could understand the importance of sharing oneself in a real and genuine way with others as a means of overcoming loneliness and boredom."

Toward Restoration of Wholeness

You may find a restoration to wholeness through a variety of methods, or you may wallow in the mire of self-pity. The temptation to self-pity strikes everyone at times; and after the loss of a spouse, you may feel you can indulge in the luxury of it. But such is debilitating. It is a destructive, negative emotion that should not be tolerated for long. You can always see that there are other people who live with worse circumstances or that you are not alone in facing a situation with which others seem able to cope. Best of all, you may determine that you are not going to permit the termite of self-pity to eat away the vitality of your personhood.

Marge affirms, "Boredom is something I haven't had much trouble in experiencing. Loneliness is one feeling I try to ignore. When I feel it coming, I usually pick up the phone and call a friend or go visit one or go someplace where there are a lot of people. Counting my blessings helps also."

Why not count your blessings in spite of? What about looking at what you have left instead of dwelling on what you have lost? This is not to suggest that we should not meditate upon pleasant memories from the past. Singles again have many assets. Usually they are healthy and often they are young, with much time ahead. They have enough character to build upon and can make a solid contribution to society. And then—there is hope, enough to pull us out of the mire of self-pity.

The battle of routine may be exhausting, but there is therapy in work (not overwork, but enough work). If one has not already learned the art, now is a good time to begin living one day at a time. Time is a great healer if we relax enough to give it a chance. In this period of readjustment, one should spend a great deal of thought on how to be more human in getting along with people. Practice the art of being kind to others and sensitive to their needs. Your need of acceptance will be fulfilled, and others will find you attractive.

Perhaps you can discover a friend or two who can fill the niche in the manner expressed thus: "O, the comfort, the inexpressible comfort, of feeling safe with a person, having neither to weigh thoughts nor measure words, but pouring them all out, just as they are, chaff and grain together, certain that a faithful hand will take and sift them, keep that which is worth keeping, and then with a breath of kindness, blow the rest away."

59

5
Coping with
the Stigma of Divorce

Unfortunately there is still some stigma about divorce. People often talk of divorce as "breaking up the marriage" or "breaking up the home.". They are referring to the legal divorce. There are, however, several other aspects of divorce. I've already referred to affectional divorce that centers around the problem of a deteriorating marriage. The affectional divorce may have been over long ago.

Other Phases of Divorce

The economic divorce involves the division of property, child support, and possible alimony. The custodial divorce involves child custody and visitation rights. Sometimes the legal custody is different from actual custody. Legal custody refers to the person who shall have the right to govern, control, or manage the child or children. Actual custody occurs when someone having legal custody places the child in the custody of someone else. There may be split custody, one child with one parent and another child with the other parent. Or there may be joint custody where both have custody or temporary custody, which means just that. Both the custody and visitation rights present problems of support and plans for holidays and vacations.

The ritualistic divorce refers to the legal formalizing of all that has been agreed to by the parties and marks the legal dissolution of the marriage. Some are now using religious rituals in the termination of the marriage.

Psychological divorce occurs when the person is separated mentally from the personality and influence of the ex-spouse. This involves what we have called "restoration to wholeness." We have to learn to live without someone to support or someone to lean on. We must come again to depend upon ourselves and our own capacity to cope with our surroundings, with people, and with our inner selves.

Stigma in the Community

There *is* the community divorce, and this is where the stigma usually lies. It involves friends, fellow church members, and others of the community. Aside from relatives, and sometimes including them, these folk fall into three categories:

1. *The curious.* Jim relates: "In counseling with me, I think you prepared me for almost everything I have had to face. I am lucky to have had such good advice. The one thing that I've noticed over and over that I didn't think much about happening is how insensitive and nosy people are. They will ask me just about anything; but I've developed a special talent for getting around just about any question they might ask."

The curious may be surprised at the divorce, but are more preoccupied with and eager to learn about the settlement. They may seem to find pleasure in the suffering of the people involved and wonder if they should continue their friendship. They are usually tolerant or indifferent as far as morals are concerned and often are envious of the freedom that they feel the divorced person has. Sometimes there are aspirations for sexual relations and fantasies even to the point of propositioning the divorced person or the person in the process of getting a divorce.

2. *The condemners.* In their "anxiety" over the situation, they gossip. "Oh, isn't it awful!" Sometimes they make requests at prayer meeting and spell out some of the sordid details, or they whisper as though there were a great deal of shame attached. They are inordinately preoccupied with moral issues. "Who's to blame?" They may feel superior. To many in this

group, marriage failure is an unpardonable sin. Someone has said, "The army of the Lord is the only one where some have the policy of shooting the wounded." Ashley expressed it this way: "I feel both at work and church that people think I'm dirty. Wives seem to dislike me very much. No one sits with me at my church and I have nearly left many times to join another one; but I've been at _____ since my teens, and my children know only this church. My sixteen-year-old daughter is active in all of the youth programs. I attend another church on Sunday nights. I wish more people would realize that this could happen to them. We don't know when we'll get traded in for a newer model, do we?"

3. *The concerned.* While these may feel conflicts over allegiances to the parties involved, they experience a sense of loss and grief along with the persons being divorced. There is a real empathy and acceptance of the persons with warmth and supportive affirmation.

Understand the Stigma

"Sticks and stones may break my bones, but words will never hurt me." But they do!

What do you do when your community ostracizes you? your friends walk out of your life? your church seems to forget you? These questions were raised in a brochure of a divorce adjustment seminar. Dr. James Travis, chaplain, University Medical Center, Jackson, Mississippi, addressed the seminar group and said in part:

"First you try to understand: Why the stigma? Now that won't make the poster-board feeling of being all alone in the world go away, but man learned a long time ago that to name the demons makes them seem less threatening to his life. So we can name at least three of the major factors accounting for divorce stigma in our society.

"We can label one the *moralistic reason.* In established religion in our culture and our society, all forms, there has often occurred the rigidity that loses sight of the continuing creativity of God. We should not be locked into certain outmoded, obsolete ways of thinking. These may well have served their purpose once upon a time but now simply lose out in trying to interpret and reinterpret the age-old gospel to a new and modern world. Such religion has translated holding people accountable for their actions, which is well and good, into condemning them for their sins. The biblical injunction against divorce has been isolated from the many more frequent statements about forgiveness.

"Those who hold such rigid views read in the New Testament all the many references to a loving, inclusive approach of God in his Christ. They pass over them to those few Scriptures which zero in on some parts of our lives in judgment, and they really get the mileage out of them. I am not suggesting that we delete anything. I'm simply saying that we need to put things in their perspective. And the moralistic reason for this stigma in our society against divorce and divorcees, more painfully, is that it has had a hard time putting things in perspective."

Jesus never condoned the woman taken in adultery. What he did was merely remind the crowd, and rather graphically at that, that sin is a pervasive part of our lives and that everybody needs forgiveness.

A second reason for the stigma is *social*. Morality and society are closely linked together. In our world today there are certain social factors which help throw up a stigma against divorcees. Ours is a couple-oriented society, and a single again often feels like a fifth wheel. Without approaching this society as part of a couple, you simply get left out of a lot of things. There is also a symbolic threat about divorce. The very existence of someone who has been through the process demonstrates the possibility of ending existing marriages and may actually be felt as a threat. Divorcees are potentially alternate spouses for ones already married.

"While society permits divorce, we haven't done very much about institutionalizing ways of helping the divorcees. We have been very inadequate in catching up with some of the liberty and the freedom that we at least give lip service to; and this is the subtle bind that our social structures have created for us. We have made it about as easy as possible, given all other factors in our world, for two people to dissolve in the courts their marriage relationships; but let them do that and listen to the consequences they face.

"A third reason for the stigma is *legal.* Divorce has not always been a concern of the courts. Back in earlier times it was primarily church officiated. Church marriages were church recognized, and in rare instances the dissolution of that marriage was allowed by the church. But with the separation of church and state, divorce increasingly became a matter for the courts. And so under the court system there was set up the structure familiar to the courts. There is a technical word for it—the adversary system—which in court lingo means that somebody has done something that they ought not to have done. There is a guilty party. Sometimes, even worse than that, the divorce conflict may become more pronounced with this legal process. You know, the more you vie with each other to get all that you can and not give any more than you have to, there often comes untold hurt and damage to both parties and children, if any. Now many states have a 'no fault' divorce law which tends to avoid some of this trauma by allowing for the possibility of legally dissolving a marriage that is already broken by other than the adversary system.

"Naming the demon doesn't make him go away, but it helps us to know who he is. But the big question is: What is our response to the stigma that our society sets up around us?"

Destructive Responses

"There are some destructive responses that you should avoid. First, avoid proving that the stigma is warranted by a *don't care* attitude, something of a self-fulfilling prophecy. When you tell folks long enough how bad they are, sooner or later they are going to fall in line with that way of thinking. So it could be that a *don't care* attitude on the part of those who have undergone the trauma of divorce may well warrant at least some of the stereotypes. Like most stereotypes in our world, there is always some measure of truth in them, such as sexual irresponsibility, cruelty, and thoughtlessness. When we adopt this attitude and fall into these patterns without really giving thought to our responsibility, then we make a destructive response by proving that the stigma is right. We play out the role. 'Well, if that's what they think of me, if I'm going to get blamed for it anyway, I may as well . . . whatever.' That's one no-no.

"The second destructive response is out-self-righteousing the self-righteous. 'If you can't beat 'em, join 'em!' or 'Beat them at their own game.' This is the idea of becoming a mirror that reflects the same spirit of bitterness and rigidity that has helped create the stigma that divorces have to face in the first place. So—a second no-no.

"A third, and perhaps more frequently used destructive response, is a form of self-pity and retreat. This is accomplished by our moving with the pressures of the stigmas so as to let them cheat us out of relationships that are rightfully ours— relationships in our clubs, neighborhood, and church. This response is making the decision by default. It is living one's life on the defensive. Thus by pitying yourself because no one has had it as badly as you, you let a lot of your life go by."

Creative Responses

"First, let this experience be an exercise in *intentionality*. Exercise initiative. Go on the offensive with your life rather than the defensive. This is exactly contrary to what I have just labeled as self-pity and retreat. Inasmuch as you can (and granted, it may be terribly limited at times), you must take the initiative and assume responsibility for your life. Now the circle within which you do that may be small, *but you do it!* Granted that blind, thrashing action doesn't always help, it is important to *do* something.

"I am much more impressed with the power of positive acting than with the power of positive thinking. Do not let your friendships die by default, even if discussing the break is painful. Get the issue out into the open. You are moving in the same circles, doing the same things, but you sense uneasiness in a very good friend. You feel the 'withering' of friendship beginning. Don't just sit there moaning and groaning. Address the issue openly. It may mean going to the friend and saying, 'I know what's happening and how things are. You do, too. We've been friends a long time. I want you to know that our friendship is important enough to me not just to sit by and see it die because I no longer have a wife/husband.' This is no guarantee that you won't still lose the friendship, but the fact is that you may well not lose it because you have demonstrated enough stamina and caring to address the matter head-on. And I do believe that even the loss of such a friendship will not be as ragged and as damaging to your own selfhood as if you just sit by and watch it die. You know deep down that you have done what you could.

"The second creative response is: Do not personalize the stigma any more than you have to. That's why naming the demon and trying to figure out the whys may help. Stigma is attached to divorce regardless of individual situations. This means that we are not to work at feeling guilty so as to fit into the divorcee role. We burn up a lot of energy in helping ourselves feel guilty; and if it doesn't come out directly associated with the divorce itself, it may well find expression in other avenues of life. We become overly conscious about it if the kids happen to be in our custody—about whether we do the right thing about here, there, and yonder. Sometimes we become overly conscientious in our work, like the common cry of parents whose children get into difficulty, 'What did I do wrong?' This idea of taking the guilt ourselves is based on the assumption that has been drilled into us from knee-high: 'If I want the world to love me, I must be a nice person.' That is true only up to a point. But the rest of the harsh truth is that if you are a divorcee, a part of the stigma you face is toward divorcees in general and not you in particular.

"So don't take all of the responsibility upon yourself for the stigma. You say, "Yes, but that is easier said than done.' That's right; but I have said it and it may just be that you can do it. That is not to say that you get off scot-free. But in terms of creative responses, do accept responsibility for your sinfulness. Be appropriately penitent and accept God's forgiveness for who you are, where you have been, and what all you have done. It may just be that the pain of stigma will expose some of the hypocritical attitudes with which we all live, divorced or not, the kind of cover-ups that mask how we really feel and what we really think. And it could just be that when we labor under the pain of this particular stigma we might find a little more honesty about ourselves and about life than if we did not have the pain. We can discover that acceptance and grace does not depend on our perfection. Rather, it depends on an openness to life, a willingness to receive the gifts of grace whenever and wherever they come to us.

"The fourth creative response: Seek help, professional and otherwise. Divorce is a major crisis in our life, and no small part of it is the stigma that is placed by society on us. So in suggesting these ways for you to respond to this burden, I do not intend to imply that you can go it alone. The stigma itself comes from society, from the world in which we live. Consequently, you must find within the social, cultural, and religious structures of your life some means of coping with it. You don't just reach up in the sky and get it."

As we shall do later, Dr. Travis pointed to community resources available for coping with the pain of the stigma as well as other adjustment problems. Thank you, Dr. Travis, my good personal and professional friend. You have said it well!

The Children and Stigma

Ben was alarmed about his daughter. "There's a lot of class consciousness in our church," he said. "Becky is not 'in.' She wants to be included and has tried several things but backed away when she felt shut out."

To our dismay, not only do many adults view divorced people as strange or sinful and keep their distance from them; but they teach their children to think of a divorced person's child in the same way. Children sometimes make critical and cruel comments to children of the divorced. As a defense mechanism these children of the divorced may lie about the absence of the other parent and are fearful that the truth may be discovered. They feel strange in the situation. The parent, then, has the obligation to teach his child that he is not strange, sinful, or especially different from other children simply because his parents are divorced. He should be taught to be himself and to earn the respect of others. He should be reminded that he can be just as happy as anyone else and is probably happier than many children whose parents are still living together.

Sometimes children are ashamed of their parents and consequently have bad feelings concerning themselves. That is, they are ashamed of the reasons that led to the divorce, such as a drinking parent, one who has been imprisoned, a mother who has gone out with other men, or mental disease. Children should be taught that while it is natural to feel sad about these things, they are not less worthy as persons and are not bad because of something that their parents have or have not done.

Easing the Stigma with Relatives

How will relatives, members of the extended family, and even friends react when they learn of an impending divorce? A great deal depends upon when the news is broken and to whom. Usually, before a divorce, some counsel has been received from a pastor, business associate, or attorney. It would be much better if both parties would agree as to when news of the impending divorce would be announced and let it be done in a way that would not embarrass either party. It is certainly not necessary for either person to spread emotional germs over the business or social community. Sometimes it is more difficult to tell relatives, especially parents, about marriage sickness or failure than someone outside the family.

One's Own Parents

There is much variation in the relationship between persons and their own relatives. One of the chief hazards in this relationship is the possibility of reverting to childhood roles. The parents may encourage this by resuming habit patterns used in the growing-up days. Sometimes parents can develop methods or ways to help the single again achieve more independence, particularly in satisfactory living arrangements. However, in a pending divorce, one's own parents may add to the confusion of an already emotionally upset person by giving advice that is not consistent with good judgment, such as saying, "You may be happy in your decision, but the children will never get over it." They may be completely overlooking the untenable situation the children are now in.

Mature Relationships

Perhaps maturity is the key factor as to whether in-laws help or hinder, meddle or mend, in a given situation. Just as weddings are family affairs, so are the disruptions of the marriages and established families. You must seek to exercise mature judgment to keep your own family relationships and those of your children at the most mature level. Your relatives may be critics, crutches, conciliators, counselors, or cushions. You must bear in mind that as far as your responsibility is concerned, children are more important than relatives, who may have to be kept at a distance when basic decisions are made, especially as regards any stigma in a divorce situation.

6
Coping with
Health and Money Matters

Why this special section on health? After all, isn't self-preservation the first law of life, and should we not all give adequate consideration to our health? Yes, we are concerned, but often we do not express this concern in tangible ways. Certainly your future is going to be affected by your physical health.

Food

Solos, both widowed and divorced, go through periods when they are not bothered with eating. "I have no appetite." "I can't get up the courage to eat by myself." "I don't like to cook for just one person or for myself and the children."

Children are very satisfied with hamburgers, and there is no real incentive to prepare balanced meals. Men are seldom trained to be good cooks. They find it easier to skip the meal. On the other hand, some singles feed their frustrations. When people are anxious, depressed, or sexually frustrated, they often turn to food as a solace. Need it be said that one should try to eat regular meals at regular times? Skipping a meal often is a strain on the body and a cause for fatigue.

Most families are pleased when Mother takes an interest in planning, cooking, and serving food. More men are studying the art of good cooking. It would seem that time spent in mastering the art would be one of the wisest investments a parent could make, especially a working mother. Not only would it save time and money; but it would provide much enjoyment for her family, as good cooking satisfies more than hunger for food.

Medical and Drug Needs

Good health involves more than good diet. Attention is usually given to dental hygiene and checkups. If these cannot be afforded on a private basis, the county health services should be utilized. The same is true for annual physical checkups. It is our observation that unless company policy demands it, persons often neglect to have regular checkups, for they have to get off from work. This should be as much a necessary routine in the average family as any other.

Some singles again find that previous health problems have been accentuated by the stress situations. Others find personality maladjustments accentuated. Still others are oversolicitous for their children as to diet, exercise, and medicine and create an overdependency or concern. For adults, there may be the hazard of a crutch such as tranquilizers, alcohol, antidepressants, and other drugs.

One should assume a responsible attitude for all prescription drugs. At least six things should be considered: (1) Take drugs only upon the prescription of a doctor; (2) take them only as prescribed; (3) do not share your prescription with someone else; (4) do not take someone else's prescription except on the doctor's advice or consent; (5) keep them stored in a locked cabinet; (6) throw away old prescriptions. It is very important for the single again to look after himself because there is no longer a spouse to nurse him during an illness.

Emotions and Health

It would be very difficult for anyone to define "normal." Usually we think of emotions or feelings in terms of negative and positive. One criteria of normalcy has been stated as: (1) free of symptoms, (2) unhampered by mental conflict, (3) having a satisfactory working capacity, and (4) being able to love someone other than himself. The single again might well say, "Well, I have my children to love, but that is about as far as I can go, though I do have to work and seem to get along fairly well."

One set of rules for happiness might read: (1) have something to do, (2) have someone to love, (3) have something to look forward to, (4) have someone to talk with about things that matter, and (5) be able to achieve at something. Again, most people would not have a 100 percent batting average.

At times each person has some of the following negative emotions, either transitory or for longer periods:

1. Anxiety over health, comfort, or property
2. Anger or hate
3. Incompetency or dependence upon others for help
4. Fear of losing control, either over oneself or the children
5. Depression or despondency with the feeling of "What's the use?"
6. Feeling of estrangement and of being misunderstood; loneliness
7. Extreme fatigue and exhaustion and a feeling of being hemmed in on every side
8. Guilt feelings and shame for being less than one thinks he ought to be or could be or, perhaps, for having failed.

You are aware that from the point of view of your children and your fellow workers, you should be considerate, efficient, dependable, and reasonable. This is very difficult to do if you harbor some of these negative feelings. Consider some results of such negative expressions. One writer has called those who enjoy thinking about their hates "adrenalin addicts."

It is not my purpose to make a psychological analysis of various types of neurotic or negative behavior, but rather to suggest that you must be careful lest you find yourself in some of these patterns that could damage physical and mental health. It is possible to analyze yourself to a certain extent, especially your negative reactions, and try to behave in a more positive fashion. Some say, "Well, I feel like sitting down and crying." Perhaps this is what is needed! Others might need more than a crying spell. A full-scale tantrum could get anger and hostility out in the open where it could be seen. Whatever is done, stop hurting yourself or your children by negative feelings and attitudes. Buck admitted, "Sometimes the bitterness really got to me, but finally I saw that I had to make some kind of life for my daughter (now sixteen) and myself, so I got busy in PWP and a Sunday School class for formerly married persons and stopped feeling sorry for myself—some." One should seek medical help and counsel, including psychiatric care if necessary. Such can be secured through mental health services if one cannot afford a private psychiatrist. Seeking psychiatric aid does not mean one is crazy. There should be no stigma attached to the idea. If you have a toothache, you go to your dentist. If you need psychiatric care, you go to a psychiatrist. It is that simple. Only a very immature or distraught person will react to the doctor's or counselor's suggestion that they see a psychiatrist with, "So you think I'm crazy!"

Hostility and Health

How one learns to handle his hostilities really makes a difference. Dr. S. I. McMillen states it this way:

> The moment I start hating a man, I become his slave. I can't enjoy my work anymore because he even controls my thoughts. My resentments produce too many stress hormones in my body and I become fatigued after only a few hours' work. The work I formerly enjoyed becomes drudgery. Even vacations cease to give me pleasure. It may be a luxurious car that I drive along the lake fringed with the autumnal beauty of maple, oak and birch, but as far as my experience of pleasure is concerned I might as well be driving a wagon in mud and rain. The man I hate hounds me wherever I go. I can't escape his tyrannical grasp on my mind. When the waiter serves me porterhouse steak, french fries, asparagus, crisp salad and strawberry shortcake smothered with ice cream, my teeth chew the food and I swallow it, but the man I hate will not permit me to enjoy it. . . . The man I hate may be many miles from my bedroom, but more cruel than any slave driver. He whips my thoughts into such a frenzy that my innerspring mattress becomes a rack of torture. The lowliest of serfs can sleep, but not I. I really must acknowledge that I am a slave to every man on whom I pour the vials of my wrath.[1]

Hostility often comes from a feeling of not being loved. One has been frustrated, rejected, neglected, and suffers from injured self-esteem. The hostile person sometimes desires vengeance and misdirects his aggressive drive. In normal people, the aggressive drive is usually as strong as the sex drive. Resentment and jealousy are special forms of hostility. Their roots are in feelings of insecurity and inadequacy. The rejected husband or wife may direct these feelings toward the person (real or imagined) to whom the "ex" has turned. Resentment may be felt about responsibility for children or from feeling tied down while the other seems to be free.

Some coping suggestions:

1. Remember that hate will destroy *you* rather than the one toward whom it is directed.

2. Others may have rejected you, but God hasn't.

3. Ask God to help you handle your emotional pain. Don't condemn yourself for having it.

4. Work off some anger feelings by physical exercise. Burn up some adrenalin.

5. A fear of the unknown could be part of the hostility. It may help to remember that we only have one day at a time.

6. Accept your temporary limitations and believe that they, too, shall pass.

7. Be grateful for what you have that is good.

8. Remember that as a person of worth, you have something valuable to contribute to family, friends, and others.

9. Think of positive actions you may take toward someone for whom you have no obligation—a neighbor, fellow church member, fellow worker.

10. Reexamine your goals. Set some new ones you may attain in a brief time.

11. Get busy changing those circumstances that need changed. Make new friends, participate in new church activities, get a new job or train for one.

12. Do not dwell on those people or situations that make you feel anger, resentment, or jealousy. Change the channel. Deliberately switch to other thought patterns that are pleasant, constructive, or positive.

Coping with Anxiety

All people face anxiety at some time in life. Everyone knows the feeling of being anxious. It is close to fear; yet when we fear something, we usually are aware of what it is. When we are anxious, we do not always know the cause. Anxiety is a state of mind which may range from vague uneasiness to unbearable emotional distress. It may be caused by fear based on mistaken religious concepts of a vengeful, cruel God, rather than a heavenly Father who loves us and desires our happiness.

Not all singles again face anxiety simply because of their new status. Many will find kinship with Edith who related, "Being divorced was like having my life given back to me again. I have never regretted my divorce. My ex-husband was an emotionally unstable, brutal, and possessive man, and I truly lived in fear the nine years I was married to him." Or your experience may be similar to that of Lois: "I had major surgery during the 'almost' year of my separation. That was a bad year physically, mentally, and emotionally; but since the divorce took place (six months after surgery) I have been healthier, have felt better, and have been in a better frame of mind than during eight years of marriage. Tension was killing me before the divorce."

The single again is often prone to anxiety, which may produce physical symptoms. An unrelieved state of tension floods the bloodstream with adrenalin and makes the nerves taut. When unrelieved, doctors tell us that ulcers, heart disease, and other ills may result. Many anxieties result from just living, others from stress situations. Neurotic anxiety gives the most trouble because the individual cannot identify the thing he fears since it is hidden from him. Psychiatrists say that one of the most common causes is repressed hostility or anger. This unexpressed rage expresses itself through depression and fatigue, irritability, and self-depreciation.

Dr. Smiley Blanton states it thus:

It is all a matter of degree. Some people are subjected to more pressure than others. Some people have stronger defenses than others.

Self-knowledge is one great line of defense. Religious faith is another. The serenity of a deeply religious faith is another. The serenity of a deeply religious person in the face of affliction is something that all of us have witnessed and admired, and the source of such serenity is clear. The person does not feel that he is facing a hostile world alone. He can shift some of the burden on a Power far stronger than himself. I have always thought that St. Paul gave some profoundly valid psychiatric advice when he wrote: 'Having done all, stand.' Do the best you can, he was saying, and leave the rest to God. Angels, themselves, could do no more.[2]

Sleep

Do you worry when you can't sleep? Most of us are too concerned about this condition. Sleep is not the only form of rest, and sleep requirements vary for different individuals. However, insomnia can be a sign of depression. Sometimes medical help is indicated. Often a study of your rest patterns may be needed. Each person develops his own patterns of shuffling off the cares of the day and allowing the pleasant feeling of lethargy to steal over him. You may like to read or listen to quiet music. You may find release in prayer or Bible reading. A few quiet moments with each one of the children and then time alone before bedtime could help. There is release in thanking God for the privileges and opportunities of the day and for his comforting care during the night.

Avoiding Work Tensions

Alice Skelsey, in her book *The Working Mother's Guide to Her Home, Her Family, and Herself*,[3] suggests four basic rules for keeping a presentable house and a reasonably organized family: (1) Do the dailies first. Every member of the family ought to be taught: "Don't put it down; put it away." (2) Plan a hunk of time for regular cleaning above and beyond the dailies. This could be a small hunk each day or two or three larger hunks weekly. (3) Never lose a day to the schedule if you can help it. You will not be tired out by it and will have a presentable house most of the time. It may not be scrupulously clean, but it won't always be messy either. (4) Don't ever in a sudden burst of energy tackle a job that you cannot retreat from and still leave the house reasonably intact—such as deciding that your closets are in terrible shape and you must clean them all that day.

Rest periods from the work are necessary to avoid tension. For a woman particularly, this might include making a brief phone call to a friend. However, if too much time is consumed, it may bring added pressure to get a job accomplished by a certain deadline and produce more tension.

One could take advantage of the odd moments. These are the times when we have to wait on some member of the family or find ourselves detained in a traffic jam. If one can learn to relax and relieve tension at this point, it will be a profitable exercise.

Relaxing from Work

Certainly it is necessary to learn to relax. Many people start as soon as they leave the office to drive home. Those who use public transportation say it is possible to relax while riding the bus. Others find it necessary to get home and change clothes or take a quick shower. A fifteen-minute rest on the bed immediately after returning home from work will "work miracles" for some.

Recreation reduces tension and therefore fatigue. There is something about physical involvement that gives relief from emotional tension of the day's activities. When we tie our worries to a physical task, often the worries recede, giving the mind a chance to rest. Outdoor exercise is an especially good antidote for worry, anger, or other debilitating emotions.

Some find relaxation in travel, even a one-day jaunt. Variety stimulates interest and curiosity.

Every person needs time to be alone. This is true for both children and parent. Private time is important for one's mental and physical health.

Money Worries

Eloise sets the stage for many: "Worry, worry. I want to move back with my family in Kentucky, but have no job and no home now. After my first divorce, I worked at odd jobs and did without a lot of necessities, but I did that before the divorce. Money has been a big problem in both marriages. My second husband was supporting two families. After six and a half years, I resented having to still support myself. He now has money, and I have to support my three children."

Georgette finds herself in a similar situation. "I worked and fed my second husband while he went to law school at night for three years. I really have been alone, although married seemingly all my life. I want to go to school and get some college, but I can't because I have to work and support myself and my three sons. If I had more college I could make more money for the hours I work. I see no end. Everyone tells me how attractive and smart and what a hard worker I am and that I can make it. I take it day by day and wish the future could be better; but no matter how hard I work, it seems when the good time is about to come, everything is lost and I'm left with nothing but three sons and their needs to meet. And I must sacrifice my wishes again. I'm now thirty-eight, but I won't give up."

Exactly What Is Your Financial Status?

As a single again, the foremost problem is to determine your exact status. Try to put it all down on paper. What are your assets? This may include house, other real estate, income, bank accounts, savings accounts, insurance (or cash value of insurance policies), stocks, bonds, accounts or notes receivable, Social Security payments, and annuities. Then look at your obligations—mortgage or notes due, car payments, insurance loans, education loans where parent has cosigned, installment contracts, and so forth. Now look at your needs in the light of the changed circumstances. Questions such as these should be asked:

1. Have housing needs changed? location as to job or school? cost of maintenance? advisability of selling, buying, renting? possibility of supplementing income or reducing expenses in such adjustment? taxes? insurance?

2. What about your health and hospitalization insurance now?

3. Automobiles—need two? one as big?

4. Home safety and upkeep, burglar proofing, yardman, maid service?

5. Income taxes, Federal and state?

6. How are you affected now by Social Security taxes?

7. Budget adjustments? Food; clothing; medical and dental care, including drugs; installment payments; allowances for the children; transportation; extra clothes and extra help; insurance payments; dues; church contributions; snacks; gifts; barber and beauty care; household help; child care; higher food costs (if woman works outside the home and for man who eats out more often); school tuition and supplies; cleaning; home furnishings; repairs; yard upkeep; automobile insurance, license, repairs, maintenance; vacation expenses; Christmas; trips; savings; and any long-range goals necessitating special funds.

Linda Lawson in *Life as a Single Adult* (Nashville: Convention Press, 1975) has an excellent budget outline on pages 20–21. Another excellent source of help is the state stewardship department of your denomination.

Dollar Stretchers

A budget is telling your money where to go rather than wondering where it went. The budget involves careful planning, but should be kept flexible, simple, and practical. Certain techniques for handling money may be noted:

1. Avoid impulse buying. Make need lists and go by them.

2. Question every dollar. Is this trip necessary? this coffee break? this item? Can a used item suffice?

3. Compare prices and learn about quality. Shop for money and insurance. Avoid high-rate interest contracts. Purchase standard models. Avoid the gadgets.

4. Do what you can yourself—sew, bake, repair, wash car, mow lawn, make Christmas gifts. (But be sure you can.)

5. Plan inexpensive recreation that you and your friends enjoy.

6. Keep good records. Develop a simple system to save time.

7. Avoid multiplicity of charge accounts. Pay by check when possible in order to have both records and receipts. Try to live within your income. There must be a payday someday! Installment buying becomes wrong when the payments control you instead of your controlling the payments. Further, it is ethically wrong to contract for something without the payments being within the realm of possibility.

Family Cooperation

Remember that family finance involves family cooperation. This requires information to the family as to your financial condition, as well as family needs and goals. Spending habits may be questioned and revised. It should not be embarrassing to say, "We can't afford it." Perhaps you identify with Joy, who said: "I have learned to do without many things, but I have also learned how unimportant things really are."

Your Children and Money

Whatever support the father gives should be known by the children, but they should not be led to feel that Dad is only "Mr. Money Bags." Help them understand that both parents are glad to do things for them, but that both, unless unusually blessed financially, will find it necessary to say, "I (or we) cannot afford that." Money should never be treasured only for itself, but thought of as a means for achieving purposes and goals. It should never be used for buying affection. Some children of divorced parents feel other children have more things than they do. These feelings may lower the child's self-esteem and must be handled wisely by the parent with whom he lives. He may identify with the "no-good" father rather than the "hardworking, self-sacrificing" mother. She should seek to picture the father with his good traits without denying his defects. After all, she once married him! The truth about the absent parent, perhaps, may best be presented gradually so that the child or youth may grow to accept him/her as a person with both strengths and weaknesses like all humans.

After the death of a parent or a divorce the child wonders, *What is going to happen to us now?* and then, *What is going to happen to us if something happens to you?* He needs reassurance at the point of economics as well as emotional security.

Money Management

Most of the trouble over money results from the way it is handled rather than the amount involved. A good credit rating is one's best asset. Honesty and reliability are the keys. One cannot afford to be slovenly or slipshod about payment of accounts or bills. Worrying over money may be wasted energy, but intelligent planning and dedicated time devoted to finances can save a lot of pain.

Rosemary has the right idea: "I keep an extremely tight budget and rarely deviate from it." Money should be used to smooth the family path and to make life easier for all. This type of management involves family understanding and agreement. While it will not be a cure-all, it will help answer the question: "What is going to happen to us now?"

Some resources for better money management:

Your banker
Voluntary health and welfare agencies such as Family Service Agency and Visiting Nurse Association
Department of Welfare and Department of Health—city, county, state
Religious denomination pamphlets and materials on stewardship and money management such as the Family Life Enrichment Series of 1977 on Money Management and Southern Baptist Convention Stewardship Department materials.

7
Coping with
Sexual Needs and Tensions

Joan's favorite chapter

"Sometimes I think I'll just climb the wall, but I still believe that someone will come along who will love me for *me.*"

"I don't want to be a bad person, but I get so hungry for love—and all I get is sex. Someone comes along who seems to respect me and considers me a person, and I just melt. I don't seem to be able to help it. Then I find I am just being used again. It's a horrible feeling. But then the first thing I know I have turned around and the same thing happens again."

"You know I have my standards. I have high morals (according to her values). But I like him a lot. I'm relaxed with him. Sex is better with him than with _____. But how do I know he will treat me right if we marry? Do you suppose he won't trust me because we have had sex before marriage? Maybe I won't trust him either. But it is so much fun with him now."

Those who are now single or have never been singles again have various ideas about singles again and sex. Some who are moral, nonjudgmental, and not suspicious would not think that singles would have problems in this area or ever be promiscuous. Others assume that since the single again supposedly has been accustomed to an active sex life, this somehow would be continued. Some singles again seem to have one standard for sexual conduct for themselves and another for their teenage children.

One Viewpoint

There are those who point out that there is more permissiveness in our time and that sexual activity between consenting

82

adults should be allowed provided there is not coercion or false pretense. Those who advocate this behavior believe their conduct should not violate public decency and do not advocate indiscriminate sex relations. They admit the dangers of emotional damage and the possibility of conscience bothering one or both of the participants.

One tells of her struggle with sexual needs: "Sexual tensions have probably been the most difficult problem for me over the six-year period. I am a very warm, outgoing person who enjoyed sex in marriage and really experience many sexual feelings and tensions. I am not ashamed of this. Maybe that gives me some kind of start in coping with it. However, I do have some deep convictions that sex just because it 'feels good' is wrong. These convictions are partially religious as I recognize what the Bible says about sex. They are also practical. I really don't believe that 'selfish sex' is rewarding. I don't think the true, beautiful, and deep meanings of sex can be experienced in a casual relationship. I must admit that I have found a compromise between these two beliefs a necessity. I have had three very deep, caring relationships with men since my divorce, which eventually included a sexual relationship. As deep as they were, I still saw too many important differences between myself and the 'other' to be willing to get into another marriage—and in retrospect, I realize I was right. I experience no guilt. In another way, I cannot reconcile this with my religious beliefs, and this *is* a problem." Many, if not most, Christian people will understand her difficulty.

The Bible View

I believe the Bible implies that a couple should be mature enough to deeply love a whole person so that neither looks upon the other as a sex thing to be used.

The Bible plainly teaches that our sexuality is a gift from God. There is nothing dirty or unholy about it when properly directed. If it is made a servant of *agape* love as God intended, then it becomes a constructive force in marriage as two people demonstrate how they are motivated, how they think and act—really, what kind of people they are.

Singles Again and Sexual Frustration

"This is a tough one (sexual tension). Because of surgery I had and because of so much sex in my marriage, I did not have a desire for sex for over a year. But it came back—real big. I find the only thing that works is to be too busy to think about it, and I usually am. Also I read some, which helps—if I watch what I read."

The following observations are from counseling files and group discussion. I am simply reporting without moralizing.

1. Some deny their need for sexual gratification. "I just don't think much about it anymore. I won't date or let myself get into any situation where I might get stirred up." "I seem to have a low sex drive. I don't have the needs I hear some people talking about. I have some physical health problems that may cause some of this. Besides, I am very fatigued most of the time."

2. Others divert their energies into some activity: sewing, housecleaning, tennis, jogging, walking, reading (nonsexy material). And some add with a laugh—cold showers—but they are serious.

3. Some seek those to be affectionate with, short of sexual satisfaction.

4. Masturbation or self-pleasuring is the answer for many. Studies have shown that a very high percentage of adults masturbate; and, contrary to the myths about it, the Bible is silent on this subject. The sin of Onan, Genesis 38:8–10, does not deal with masturbation but with his failure to fulfill the requirements of Deuteronomy 25:5–10. Dr. Charles Shedd states in his book *The Stork Is Dead* (Waco: Word Books, 1972): "Masturbation is a gift of God." Perhaps one should distinguish between compulsive masturbation reflecting psychological problems, experimental masturbation which is almost universal among children, sexual tension-release masturbation practiced by

teenagers, and fantasy tension-release patterns that some adults may consider appropriate.

Dr. Samuel Southard, lecturing to a group of singles again in a divorce adjustment seminar in Jackson, Mississippi's First Baptist Church, said in part, "Masturbation is more than physical. For the single again, one can use the reality principle in imagination. This is the way it could be. There are values that may come to the mature person in imagination. Imagine yourself as a loving partner with something to contribute as a sexual person in the direction of companionship and/or procreation." He issued a warning: "Have enough sense of significance to use your own imagination. Pictures and writings of others are not as good as your own thoughts. Most of these writings are for women to tell them how to get along with beasts who are called 'men' or for men to tell them how to act on the animal level as woman is treated as a 'thing.' Many people have problems of guilt and feelings of rejection when they begin to think of themselves as sexual beings. Some singles again go from one to another to prove they are still attractive. This proves nothing except that one can be sexually active. For others, there is the problem of shaking stereotypes; but because you may have been married to a louse is no evidence that all men or women are in this class. For some, then, self-pleasuring may be the best way to handle sexual tensions."

A psychiatrist speaking before a group of Parents Without Partners said, "For one who believes in God, prayer can be a coping strategy." He concluded with: "Most of us in the adult world use subliminations very wisely in many facets of life—in our work, social life, and sexual life. Mature adults have come to the conclusion that you are not going to have complete satisfaction in all aspects of life."

Sarah Frances Anders in her excellent treatment of *Woman Alone* tells us: "One of the most interesting things I have unearthed among nonmarrieds is that more than half readily admitted to feeling some frustration sexually, but felt that, to some extent, being restricted sexually had tended to make them more creative in other areas. Sublimation was, to them, not necessarily a cramping and nonproductive experience. Very few felt a great deal of sexual frustration but three-fourths of these women believed that the church and society should be no more permissive in sexual standards for the unmarried than for the married. Once again my counseling with married indicates that marriage does not preclude sexual frustrations." [1]

Some Implications to Consider

Singles again, therefore, should be aware of some dangers. Do not get caught on a quick rebound. A person may intend to be only a compassionate and understanding friend, but the confused single again may take this for love and react inappropriately to the proferred friendship. You will be more vulnerable if the marriage relationship with your former spouse was a good one.

It is not wrong to consider someone physically or sexually attractive. To have sexual feelings or desires is not a sin. Some types of sexual fantasies are not wrong. Lust is inordinate desire or desire out of bounds, a deliberate cultivation of illicit desire. Jesus, in condemning lust, was avoiding the legalism of the Pharisees that considered woman as chattel, as a thing, and was putting the emphasis on violating her personhood rather than violating some man's property rights.

Sex between two persons outside of marriage is fraught with many hazards. There is always the insecurity and possible guilt, not knowing what commitment or emotional involvement the other person is bringing to the relationship. Sexual experiences are so much more than physical experiences that the real meaning is lost if taken out of the context of interpersonal involvement. A young woman said, "I have two married friends who have told me that they were glad to know me because I have changed their views on people who are divorced. Sherry and Kate grew up like me, thinking that all divorced people had something wrong with them. I have another single friend with whom I have had several talks about morals and our goals in life. She still can't believe my moral views are as strong as they are. She thought all divorced women hopped from one bed to another like her roommate does."

At this point, you might like to turn to Session 8, "Special Suggestions for Sessions," and, with Bible in hand, look at sexuality from a biblical perspective.

A Christian Ethic of Sexual Behavior

In his book *The Christian Response to the Sexual Revolution*, Dr. David Mace raises the question: "On what, then, are we to base our Christian standards of sex morality? Why not on the ethical teaching of Jesus? Sexual behavior falls within the sphere of human relationships, and in that area we have quite clear criteria in the Golden Rule and in the commandment to love our neighbor. Yet in all traditional Christian writings on sex morality that I have read, I cannot recall a single instance in which this basic ethical teaching of Jesus is taken as a guideline.

"It would be interesting to re-examine the whole field of sexual behaviour in the light of questions that are basic to the Christian, such as, 'What would it do to me as a child of God and a follower of Christ?' 'What would it do to my sexual partner, who is my neighbor to be loved as myself?' 'What would it do to the family and to the well-being of children?' 'What would it do to human society?' Surely these are the criteria by which the ethics of any sex act should be judged. And these are the criteria which are not only binding upon the Christian but which would readily be recognized by many responsible people who are outside of the organized church." [2]

Roger H. Crook stated it succinctly in his *Christian Family in Conflict:* "As is true for married people, unmarried persons need not look upon sex as the highest good in life. Life without sexual relations can be good, just as a sex relationship in marriage can be bad. In other words, success in life is not dependent upon the sex relationship." [3]

What does the single again do about sex? There are alternatives. Each must make his own choice and live with the consequences. A good question to ask is: "How can I fill this need in a manner by which I can maintain my self-respect?" One's background, conscience, religious beliefs, or moral convictions will help predetermine the choice.

8
Coping as
a Single Parent

There is a sense in which parental roles cannot be changed, but in most families they are often interchanged. Many men do housework or baby-sitting, and some women find themselves being chief disciplinarian or breadwinner.

Avoid a Completely Child-oriented Home

As a single parent, you may tend to be overprotective or overpermissive and allow your home to become completely child-oriented. To do so is unfair and unhealthy for all involved. Children's needs must be given high priority, but the family should still be considered as a unit and directed to meet the needs of all.

Much attention is given to boys identifying with a strong masculine figure and girls identifying with a feminine figure. There is some validity in this at certain stages of the developmental cycle. Perhaps it is more important to consider the effect of child-rearing practices on personality development. It boils down to this: Insofar as possible, do what you would do if your spouse were still with you.

One must take his child where he is in a particular stage of development and move from there. It is important for the child not to blame you, the ex-spouse, or himself for what has happened to the family and to be rid of guilt he may have acquired from the circumstances. Your own emotional adjustment to the situation is one of the strongest factors in the adjustment of the children.

Toward the Child's Maturity

Many parents have goals for their children. They are convinced that they know what is right for the child or what is right, period!

Contrast this pattern with the parent who sees the child as an individual and respects his patterns of growth toward maturity. He does not try to make the child an extension of himself but gives freedom to grow. He influences the child but does not ignore the other factors in his behavior. Discipline is based upon needs and relationships and involves more than punishment and rewards. Communication—open and free—is encouraged. At least one meal together every day helps keep the lines open. Practice making some inexpensive dinner date with one child at a time. In an informal setting apart from others, a parent is better able to listen, respect views, tactfully correct if necessary, and challenge as little as possible.

The considerate parent will allow his child to learn, being careful not to stifle initiative and respect. He will interpret and answer questions and train toward independence, self-confidence, and self-esteem.

Listen! Listen with both mind and heart to the child's interests, changing whims, serious goals, testing values, fears, joys, and triumphs. This will say to him, "I'm really with you." But this concept involves more than presence. It conveys security. It tells the child, "You belong here. We are together. We share in humor, in joy, in contentment, in serious and lighthearted moments. Whether I'm present or absent, you can count on me!"

No Parent Substitutes

Today's parents seem to feel very helpless and inadequate. More and more parenthood privileges are being delegated to others, and this often must be accelerated when the parent becomes solo. Nursery schools, day-care centers, camps, church organizations, schools, clubs, Scouts, and so forth take over.

Television baby-sitting, movies, the "Y," swimming pool, recreation center, music lessons, dancing, tennis, riding—all bring in a wide variety of outsiders.

The "activities" and "things" may become parent substitutes. No doubt they bring some enrichment to the child, but there is no substitute for shared experience with the parent to develop emotional stability in the child. He must know how the parent feels, his sense of values, how he faces joy, frustration, grief, defeat, and success. In the emotional shelter called home, the child must become acquainted with all of the significant realities of life.

With the support of parental love of one parent, your child can learn to take the bitter with the sweet. He can learn to face difficult challenges and know the joy of difficult achievements. He can learn that he is part of a community of individuals and that, as he finds satisfaction for his own needs, he cannot ignore the needs of others. He must learn to live with his own limitations and learn how to accept or at least tolerate others with their apparent weaknesses. He must learn to develop his capabilities. Thus the parent is preparing the child to cope with his own complicated feelings and a very complex world.

Single parents may be so sorely disturbed by the family disruption that they seem temporarily unfit for the task. At this point it is good to get professional help. When the disruption has come by divorce, the parent is apt to despair of giving the child what he needs for his own future happiness and well-being. But the sheltering, guiding love of *one* emotionally mature parent can be very good insurance that the child may develop his own maturity for all aspects of life, including marriage and parenthood.

To paraphrase Louise Despert in *Children of Divorce,* central heating cannot take the place of human warmth; entertainment is no substitute for human companionship; and sterile cleanliness need not shut out love. While two loving parents are most desirable, one parent can give companionship and love.

Helping Children Cope with Death

Now to some more specific considerations. What do you tell the children in event of death? We need to remember that they are well acquainted with it through the mass media. The sad facts should be presented as simply and directly as possible. Children live in feelings more than in reasoned actions. The conveyer of the news should seek to avoid communicating more anxiety and fear than the event itself will bring. He must stand by to sustain the child's first outpouring of feeling with calmness and confidence. Children should not be denied their right to grief. This is not the time for theological or rational discussions; yet there may be some questions raised that should be answered in a simple, factual manner. One must be careful not to overanswer by attaching adult meanings to a child's question.

Comforting the Child

If you have lost your spouse by death and the children are old enough to be told something about death, you should have a good understanding of the nature and expression of children's grief. Children tend to work out their feelings through their behavior which may take various forms. A child feeling deprived of something very important in his life may show his grief in anger. This expression may be rather obscure or quite evident. The child may feel that he is going to be left alone—abandoned. He seeks to keep the living parent always in sight, and smaller children may actually cling to clothing and want to hold the parent's hand all the time.

"I was ten when my daddy died. My mother was badly in need of rest, and I can remember I would not let her sleep. Every time she closed her eyes, I would climb up on the bed and wake her. I am sure, now that I'm grown, I was afraid *she* would die."

The child will certainly want to be included in any group so he can know what is going on. He must have reassurance during this time that he is loved and is not going to be left. If he is old enough to ask what will happen if the living parent should die, some sensible or reasonable statement ought to be made such as, "Grandmother and Granddaddy will take care of you" or "There are other ways that you will be taken care of so that you will not be left alone."

A child should not be forced to go to a funeral home. If he does go, be at his side to make him feel in the presence of a natural phenomenon that affects all sooner or later. Perhaps very young children should be spared the funeral. Then they can be told about death in terms of their own understanding, free from satisfied curiosity and morbid fears or the grief reaction of others. Some youngsters carry into their early teens a form of death denial, the belief that one being buried is actually still alive. This possible worry may be eased by viewing the remains of the parent or other family member who has died and by other aspects of the funeral. A child of any age does need to know that the deceased person did not "just go away," as this thought could raise fears of rejection.

At times, the surviving parent contributes to the emotional confusion of the young by deifying the dead or suddenly forgetting all his imperfections. It is more emotionally healthy to handle pent-up feelings of hostility that may have accumulated, recognize some of the contributing factors, and deal with them in terms of forgiveness.

Other children and some adults want to damn God for the death or blame God for the circumstances. This becomes a question to be dealt with in terms of the family's theological concepts and can best be handled by the family pastor. Many people within the tenets of their religious faith make a distinction between the permissive will and the directive will of God.

In the freedom God has given to man, he does not direct that one becomes incompetent to drive by drinking alcohol or taking other drugs. Nevertheless, the driver or some other person may be killed by such irresponsible action. While adults may piously rationalize, "This is God's will," this does not coincide with the concept of a God of love who wills joy but may permit sorrow.

Conveying Security Feelings

Sometimes younger children feel insecure about the parent with whom they are living. "My children want to know where I am all the time." The older child may have the same thoughts but feel responsible for the emotional well-being of the parent, especially thinking that someone should offer the parent constant companionship.

As for security, the parent's acceptance of the child even when he is least tolerable must be paramount. Acceptance tells the child he is likable, that he has worth as a person, and is capable of conveying these good feelings to others. Rejection expressed in hostile ways such as belittling, ridicule, or physical abuse causes the child to feel worthless and perhaps hopeless.

The child also finds security in proper discipline or controls. Love will set limits. The word *permissiveness* should not convey a lack of limits. By controls or limits imposed from without one becomes a disciplined person. The external controls become internalized. One can overprotect by excessive control and thus cripple the child in his ability to cope with life. On the other hand, excessive permissiveness is not normal in any social situation.

Discipline Patterns

"Consistency, thou art a jewel" was never truer than when applied to discipline. It must include what is permitted as well as what is prohibited. The child's behavior may be unacceptable, but he is never unacceptable as a person. You may have understandings as to behavior patterns; and when the understanding is violated, some form of punishment may be necessary. Understandings are better than rules with penalties already attached. How seriously your understanding has been violated plus any extenuating circumstances may be considered when no penalty is automatically attached. "We are in this together" becomes the mark of an understanding between parent and child, whereas the rule concept implies an authoritarianism that may involve disrespect for persons on either side.

Parents who practice the understanding method find less use for physical punishment and more opportunity to use reason. Lest the term be misunderstood, understanding involves an agreement between parent and child of behavior patterns acceptable to both. It involves trustworthiness and notes ability to carry out the agreement. The parent does not try to manipulate the child and thwarts the child's attempts at manipulation. Openness is desired and expected, though this does not mean accountability for every hour or event—especially as the children grow into their teen years. Privacy must be respected and safeguarded for both the parent and child.

Decision Making

There are many areas of decision making in child development—clothes, friends, recreation, budgeting, dating, vocational choice, study. Children need guidance in these choices. Often they must be allowed to make mistakes, suffer the consequences, and learn to live with their choices. They must be taught to be individuals and in some areas to be nonconformists. The parent will convey his own set of moral values and his reason for feeling as he does. However, he should guard personal prejudices he does not want his child to have. He may find it necessary to counteract unworthy community feelings his child picks up.

Community Activities

It seems more difficult for a single parent to participate in community activities, but some time should be spared for those events, projects, or organizations affecting the life of the child. A child may feel very good that "my mother is a member of the PTA." Dad should prefer to be at the Little League game with his fingers gripping the heart of his son rather than gripping a golf club while out with the "boys."

Teaching About Sex

It is proper to say that sex education began the day your child was born.

A child learns about masculinity and feminity by observing the way adults relate to each other in tenderness, affection, consideration, courtesy, kindness, and the pleasure of touch. When one comes to the actual discussion or answering questions about sexual matters, certain values should be present. One is a sense of reverence as you realize that sexuality is God-given. You are not to be ashamed or embarrassed by your sexual nature.

Questions should be answered honestly but in terms of the child's understanding at the time. However, it is better to tell too much too soon than too little too late. One should be as unemotional as possible. Sometimes parents are embarrassed by the matter-of-fact questions asked. If you evade or avoid the question, you may later be more painfully embarrassed by the ignorance of your children.

Sexual matters must not be presented in such a way as to produce abnormal fears. Granted, youth should still fear detection if there is sexual intimacy, even with the pill and/or other contraceptive devices. Fear of infection with venereal disease is still valid! However, there is nothing unholy or unclean or sinful about sex by nature. Sex is meant for union in commitment. "The two shall become one flesh" is more than a physical relationship, though procreation is one purpose of sex. The Bible teaches that there are to be no perversions. Sex is not to be a master but rather a servant. Sexual intercourse in marriage should be among the best expressions of mature love.

All of these concepts cannot be introduced at once. Usually the information is presented in a developmental pattern. Before the child goes to school he should know the facts of birth. Then a year or so before time for the daughter to menstruate, the parent should be sure there is an understanding about this. It is better a few years before than a few days after. The young man should know about nocturnal emissions (wet dreams). Before dating, the young woman and young man should know about sexual excitability and that there is logic to chastity before marriage that goes beyond any authoritarian commands. *Why Wait Till Marriage* by Duvall (New York: Association Press, 1965) contains one of the best discussions on this subject. The child should be taught that sexual intercourse is reserved for love in marriage. It involves more than "a covenant of intimacy" or "situation ethics."

There are many good resources to help parents who are concerned about these questions. Among them are: American Medical Association pamphlets, Broadman Sex Education graded series, Concordia Sex Education Series, Duvall's *About Sex and Growing Up, Love and Facts of Life,* and *Why Wait Till Marriage,* Howell's *Teaching About Sex—A Christian Approach,* and Shedd's *Letters to Karen, Letters to Phillip,* and *The Stork is Dead.* Many religious denominational press books deal with these subjects. Consult your religious book store.

Other sections that deal specifically with child-parent relationships are in chapter 4, *"The Children and Your Date,"* and chapter 5, *"The Children and Stigma."*

To My Children

What is my wish?
To be the kind of man
Who can be the kind of father
That you need
To grow strong
And to be whole.
And what you sense now
I hope you will come to understand
That my first faithfulness to you
Requires that I be faithful
To myself.
That my integrity

Is my hope
And my hope
Is my ability to love
Is my vulnerability
To you
And to all the world.
I ask forgiveness
For the pain I've caused
And I ask for the continuing gift
Of your trust.
You are for me
A special song of joy.[1]

9
Should the Single
Again Remarry?

"I certainly have no plans for remarriage; nor do I have the need. I find my life as a single very active, useful, and satisfying."

Marriage is out of the question for many widows and widowers and even for some divorced people. There is no desire to find another partner. Although this view is expressed shortly after divorce or the death of a spouse, some change their minds later. The thought of remaining unmarried may be paramount because the first marriage was so happy—or unhappy, as the case may be. If it was unusually happy, there is the fear that nothing could compare with it. If unhappy, there is the fear of another bad experience. When you love another, there is always the possibility of being hurt. By avoiding exposure, you try to protect yourself.

"I fear rejection again. I can't seem to let any man close enough to my inner feelings to consider any type of close relationship."

"I'm scared. I'm a two-time loser. I'm afraid I'll make the same mistake again. How can you know? I have a few friends I feel comfortable with. The people at church all treat me OK. I feel good there. Wonder what it is about me that makes me always fall for the wrong sort of person?"

"I may have set my standards too high. Maybe there is no one who will measure up to them, or maybe someone will come along and fool me again. But I'm going to wait and see."

"I am very happy in my single state; but if someone irresistible came along, I would consider remarriage."

"At first the thought of remarriage was negative, mostly because the biggest problem in my marriage was children by a former marriage. (Their father was deceased.) I do not want to involve my children in another situation like this. I have overcome the negative attitude and have decided that when and if I should fall in love and the feeling is mutual, I will worry about it then. Looking at it this way helps me enjoy men's company more."

To Love Again

One who has had a fulfilling relationship in marriage and has the capacity to love may soon love again. This may explain why some, after the death of the spouse, remarry more quickly than relatives think they should. Concluding that you must learn to love again, it is wise to reevaluate yourself as a person worthy of being loved. You may desire to care even though your caring may be imperfect. You may want to belong—to share with another. You perhaps want to have a warm sexual relationship. You may have some emotional capacities that have not been realized, especially if your marriage ended in divorce. You may think of yourself as an affectionate, outgoing person with the capacity to love another without making that person an extension of your own personality. You calculate that there may be possible happiness in remarriage. Love may be better the second time around.

This is a very real possibility because you may have matured, may have learned something from your first experience that will be helpful. And because you have studied yourself, you now realize your contribution to the first marriage failure. You will not want to rush into remarriage but will recognize that the second marriage will be different from the first. There are a number of differences: children involved, financial arrangements, budget, housing, wife's working, and many other adjustments that will contribute to the happiness or unhappiness in remarriage. One man summarized it: "Before one remarries, I think one should first meet someone who is compatible, one with whom he/she can communicate, and one who has like interests. Factors that should be considered are religion, money, children, jobs, insurance, wills and trusts, activities, pleasures, homes, sports, and recreation."

If there are children, several other questions must be raised. What about the other parent? What are we going to tell the child about the stepparent? What will the child call the stepparent? What will be the role of the stepparent? What about the wedding and the child or children?

"One thing I know. We have grown through the trauma of our experiences. It is not easy to put two families together. Our children probably are doing better than we are. We carry their burdens too much. When we sort out our problems we get along better; and it really helps when George and I have some time for ourselves to relax and talk about something besides problems."

Living in Step by Roosevelt-Lofas (New York: Stein and Day, 1976) deals candidly and constructively with the problems and pleasures of stepfamilies. In 1976 Ms. Lofas founded the Step Family Foundation Inc. in New York City to continue work and study in this area of family relationships. One who is stepparenting or considering stepparenting will find many helpful insights from this book's psychological and experiential view.

Do I Have a Right to Remarry?

Some have been taught that when one is divorced, he must remain single for life. There is no Bible justification for this. In Bible times it was expected that one would remarry after divorce. There was no economic pressure for a widow to remarry as she was a part of the extended family. Paul's exhortation to celibacy was in the context of his expecting the immediate return of Christ.

Your Church and Remarriage

What about your church? When one has lost his spouse by death and chooses to remarry, no question is raised by the people or the minister. If one of the persons seeking remarriage has been divorced, questions may be raised. Some church groups look askance at one marrying outside their church or denomination. Some frown upon a church member marrying a nonchurch member. No one can speak for another person, denomination, or church in this respect. However, it should be stated that no church or denomination believes in divorce as the *ideal.* But simply because many of the marriage ceremonies indicate that the persons vow to stay together for better, for worse, until death do us part, there are very few church groups that really believe there are no extenuating circumstances that make it advisable for some people to divorce— or at least separate.

Be that as it may, people do find themselves divorced. Christians do put asunder what God has joined together, though some question that God really had anything to do with their marriage in the first place. In Matthew 19:6 "What God therefore hath joined together" does not refer to *whom* except in that Jesus was saying that the original purpose of God was for the marriage union to remain indissoluble. Church members find themselves divorced, and many of these people remarry. Most desire that a minister, priest, or rabbi perform the ceremony; and many seek one who will do so.

Some denominations are recognizing divorce as a viable alternative to living in a nonlove situation by suggesting a marriage termination ceremony as a possibility.

The Minister's Decision

Some denominational groups share with the minister in making rules or regulations; however, the minister must make the decision in most cases about performing marriage ceremonies for the divorced. Some refuse to marry anyone who has been divorced and will not discuss the matter further. They announce this as their policy when moving to a new field of work. Other ministers will marry anyone who presents them with a marriage license. Still others marry divorced persons provided the one being married is the "innocent" party where there has been unfaithfulness, meaning adultery. Some ministers have found this position untenable when they discover that people will lie in order to get them to perform the ceremony, whereas others will lie because they don't want to cast any aspersions upon the former spouse.

Ministers often find themselves performing beautiful church weddings and four months later welcoming a child born to this couple. They see a rather gross inconsistency in the innocent party concept. The minister would hardly dare ask the prospective bride in this situation, "Are you pregnant?"

Obviously, there are many perplexing questions for the minister, the church, and the persons involved—such as what makes a marriage. Marriage is a commitment leading to a total way of life, a shared partnership of all of life. It is this intimate life and love of two persons that leads to their natural expression in sexual union. The physical act of marriage is not marriage itself. The marriage license is more than a legal consent to a contract for sexual activity. Christian marriage occurs when two people, male and female, covenant to give themselves to each other in *agape* love, thus sanctifying their erotic and companionable needs. The consummation of the marriage in sexual intercourse becomes symbolic of the uniqueness of their loving and sharing relationship.

Another question: What do you do with Matthew 5:31–32? Among the Jews, adultery was an act against the property rights of the husband. Fornication or unchastity among the Jews referred to incest, sodomy, bestiality, and other forms of forbidden sex acts as described in Leviticus 20:11–21.

But what about Matthew 5:32 and "living in adultery"? Adultery is an act. It would be impossible to live in adultery. According to the Scriptures, what happens between husband and wife is never called adultery—though there may be other things considered by some to be worse. Many married people living together sexually have expressed the feeling that they were being used and were sinning against each other because they were having sex without love.

Perhaps William Barclay's statement will be appropriate to consider here:

> We have to be careful what we do here (in the Matthew account—Matt. 5:32). First, we have to face the fact that sexual infidelity is far from being the only thing that can wreck a marriage. It is one of the curious facts of language that the word *immorality* has come almost exclusively to mean sexual immorality. There is many a person in marriage who is blameless from the legal sex point of view, but who has nonetheless succeeded in making marriage a hell for the other partner. Fletcher quotes a passage from Dorothy Sayers: A man may be greedy and selfish; spiteful, cruel, jealous and unjust; violent and brutal; grasping, unscrupulous, and a liar; stubborn and arrogant; stupid, morose, and dead to every noble instinct; and yet, if he practices his sinfulness within the marriage bond, he is not thought by some Christians to be immoral.
>
> There are other things than adultery which can kill a marriage and the love which should be in it.
>
> The second thing we have to be careful about is that we do not try to make the words of Jesus into a law, and thus forget that the greatest thing of all is love. We have always to remember that we have to take to any situation the *whole* of the message of Jesus, not just one sentence from it.
>
> But if it should so happen that two people find living together an impossibility; if they have consulted the doctor and the minister or the priest and the psychologist and the psychiatrist; if they have taken all the guidance that there is to take, and if the situation is still beyond mending, then I do not think that it is an act of Christian love to keep two such people tied together in a life that is a torture; nor do I think that it is right for them only to be allowed to separate and never be allowed to try to start again. In such circumstances I believe that divorce is the action of Christian love, for I do not think that Jesus would have insisted that two utterly incompatible people should be condemned to drag out a loveless existence, heartbreaking for themselves and disastrous for their children. Nor do I believe that they should be forbidden to remarry and to remarry with the blessing of the church. Nor do I think that I would wish to talk much about innocent and not innocent parties, for when a marriage breaks up I should doubt if there is any such thing as an altogether innocent and an altogether guilty party.[1]

Another Scripture that many consider is 1 Corinthians 7:12–17, where Paul suggests that divorce is permissible on the grounds of the unbeliever's desertion. The believer is not under bondage—that is, not held by constraint of law or necessity. It is the legal term used for divorce.

It would seem that Jesus may have allowed for divorce on sexual grounds and Paul on grounds of desertion, stating, "God has called us to peace" (v. 15). This must have definitely meant divorce and not separation, for the idea of separation was unknown both to the Jew and the Greek. Further, neither Jew nor Greek ever questioned the right of remarriage following divorce. Could it be that this explains why the right to remarry is not mentioned by either Jesus or Paul?

The divine norm for marriage was a monogamous relationship for life. But Dr. D. Hervey Small, respected authority in the field of marriage, states: "Grace does not compromise God's norm. Grace redeems and restores those who fail to meet God's norm. Grace has the final word. Grace is triumphant!" [2]

Dr. Lofton Hudson, writing in *Persons in Crisis,* says:

> The kind of help the divorced person needs, as he thinks through how he stands with his Christian community, is to hear them say out loud that they can believe that people can fail at marriage like they do in business, or morally, or in getting along with their neighbors; that a marriage which was once alive can die as truly as if it had been terminated by physical death; that the right to get a legal divorce is a natural presupposition for another marriage; and that it would be a sin not to remarry if the divorcée finds a sound relationship and can come nearer to being a whole person by marrying.[3]

It is too late at this point to discuss what the pastor or church should have done before the first marriage failed. There should have been premarital counseling and guidance which could have, perhaps, avoided some of the conflicts leading to the divorce. Did the pastor and church give attention to the couple during the first few years of marriage? Do the church and pastor provide a family counseling service, curriculum materials on family life, or family life conferences? When the separation came, did the church try a ministry of reconciliation? It is too late to lament. As Wayne Oates states, "The divorced Christian is a symptom of the irresponsibility of the church as a teaching community and its failure of nerve as a fellowship of human suffering."

Realized Forgiveness

Writing on the remarriage of divorcees in *Pastoral Counseling in Social Problems,* Dr. Oates presents the position that he names the "confrontational and therapeutic approach" which confronts the couple with the claims of the gospel and whatever failure has been theirs in the previous marital experience. No effort is made to fix blame or to declare guilt and innocence.[4] "For all have sinned, and come short of the glory of God" (Rom. 3:23). No one is to blame, but everyone is responsible; so guilt is not bypassed but distributed. The church and its ministry share corporately in the sin. The lack of premarital counseling, pastoral follow-up, the absence of communication when the marriage begins to flounder and at the time of separation—all of these are a shared responsibility between the church and the divorcee. In this contemplated second marriage, the church, the pastor, and the couple are facing responsibly their relationship together. This means many hours of counseling by trained people, and Dr. Oates encourages the church to see that the pastor has such training and to share with him in this type of family ministry. It is unrealistic to believe that most pastors already have training in this field. If the couple is unwilling to take this premarital approach with the pastor, then perhaps he should not perform the ceremony.

Premarital counseling in my judgment should be accepted as a pastoral privilege, whether or not there has been a previous marriage. Our attitude is determined in part by how we look at people. Upon being asked, "Do you marry divorced persons?" I reply, "No, I do not. Sometimes I perform wedding ceremonies for persons who have been divorced." I could just as well add, "I do not marry liars either. But no doubt I sometimes marry people who have lied and maybe to the person they are marrying."

I feel that the church and the minister need to deal redemptively with each individual, no matter what his past has been. To help people understand the redemptive power of God in their lives is the minister's special privilege. Those who sin and those who experience failure need to find forgiveness, acceptance, and restoration. No one is perfect. No one escapes sin or failure. All need forgiveness. Families need to be built on this basis.

Dr. Hudson summarizes these feelings: "It seems that the churches are coming to a more realistic approach to the remarriage of divorced people because they are coming to see beyond their legalistic noses that 'it is not good for man to be alone' (nor a woman) and that to prevent the happiness and growth of a good subsequent marriage would be an error if not a sin." [5]

Dr. R. Lofton Hudson writing later (1973) in *Till Divorce Do Us Part* states his feelings even more strongly:

> If Jesus were here today facing our marital situations I have no doubt that he would say, "Not only is it right for some to remarry after they have been divorced, it is downright wrong for them to stay single if they have a good opportunity to remarry and feel that they can live a more fulfilling life by entering into another intimate marital relationship. It is not my will for people to live second-rate lives. I will every man and woman to his best solution under his or her circumstances." [6]

A minister charged with interpreting the mind and attitude of Christ to others must be sure that his own attitude is Christlike. Jesus did not condone sin, but he did forgive sin and taught that those who were forgiven were in God's presence as though they had not sinned. He further taught that Christian forgiveness should be unlimited. The church is supposed to be a loving fellowship of redeemed sinners—sinners of all kinds. These who have failed—or sinned, if you prefer—are now rebuilding, finding wholeness and acceptance with each other as they are mutually mediating the grace of God to each other. It is only

107

from this point of view that some ministers can take their stance. So, from my personal view, "realized forgiveness" on the part of the couple being married is the theological or biblical basis of remarriage for the divorced.

Respect Those Who Differ

Hopefully, the single again is already part of a loving fellowship as described above or will be successful in his quest.

If, however, he finds that the minister has opposing views and does not desire to give him counsel about reestablishing his home on a solid spiritual foundation, I hope that the single again will respect the minister's convictions and conduct himself in such a way that the friendship will remain intact. He should respect the minister as being honest in his feelings and attitudes, desiring to maintain integrity, just as the single again does. But this should not prevent the single again from seeking another minister who will counsel with him.

10

Resources for Coping

You have to go on; and you have certain resources to bolster you in the task. What resources do you have within your own being?

Your knowledge of yourself. You must know something of your own physical strength and emotional toughness. You believe yourself to have a certain amount of reasoning ability so that alternatives can be considered. You know how to handle disappointment and failure up to a point. In the past you have probably developed some coping devices to do this. You know something of your own spiritual vitality. "Know thyself" is still a practical admonition.

Your experience with God. When faced with problems, people often get mad at God. Among the attitudes expressed may be these: (1) God does not know about me and does not care about me. (2) God is testing me, punishing me. (3) God has let me down. I have lived a good life. God has not held up his end of the bargain. (4) God is mad at me. (5) I don't believe in God anymore. This person is rejecting God because of circumstances that have come about. (6) If God will help me out of this, I will really serve him. This is the barter method of dealing with God.

All of these are faulty views of both God and trouble. What attitudes better correlate sound psychological concepts and biblical teachings? More mature attitudes may be expressed as follows: (1) God knows and cares about my trouble. (2) God will help me through this. (3) I may be partly responsible for this, and I will assume my share of responsibility in a realistic way. (4) I can learn something from this experience. (5) God will help me endure more than I thought I could. (6) I will never give up hope.

In the crisis of trouble and anxiety, a special kind of dependency may develop along with a definite kind of loneliness. Thus the troubling experience may take on added dimensions of a religious experience. What is your experience with God? Is he real? Is he big enough to handle your circumstances? Is he a loving God, a caring Father, and a helping God? Your experience with God may become a resource as you find with the psalmist: "God is our refuge and strength, a very present help in time of trouble. Therefore will not we fear" (Ps. 46:1). Do you believe that?

Your practice of prayer. Much of our praying is self-centered. We are constantly asking as little children. True, we are told to "ask, and it shall be given you; seek, and ye shall find" (Luke 11:9), but the most effective type of praying in times of trouble is a prayer that affirms God's presence, God's power, and God's peace. Meditation following prayer or as a part of prayer helps us to listen to God's voice. He has promised to be with us and help us. Accept his promise, for he has the power to keep it. He has promised to give you peace. "Do not be worried and upset; do not be afraid" (John 14:27, TEV).

David shared his experience in prayer: "When I became single, I had three young children to raise. There was no one but myself to do this, even though I had quite a few friends. I prayed to God to relieve me, telling him that I had a big job to do in raising the children. He answered my prayer as if by a miracle, and I raised the children right. I am quite happy and they are, too. I am no fanatic on religion, but I know if one puts his heart into it God will surely help. I prayed and it happened very quickly. My mind was more at ease; and I could concentrate on my work, my activities, and raising my children. Just kneel down and have a heart-to-heart talk with God and mean it. He will help you."

110

Your practice of Bible reading may be a resource. When in trouble, one does not read the Bible to learn facts or to store up historical information. The Bible is read for listening, for seeking to hear what God says. "Be still, and know that I am God" (Ps. 46:10). Read the Bible for direction and guidance. You may not find a special passage that will exactly describe your situation, but the Bible does lay out certain principles that may give you direction. Practice reading the Bible for worship. Worship may be defined as a reverential response to the presence of God. Devotional Bible reading induces such a response.

You may strengthen your inner self by *going to church.* Some people find it helpful to go to church to pray. Some have practiced praying while kneeling in the church, finding special solace in such prayer posture. Many find strength from the minister's prayers, while others find strength in repeating ritual prayers to which they are accustomed. Others go to church to meditate. They discover that this is a good place to clear cobwebs out of their minds. They find peaceful relaxation. Creative thinking is often stimulated by a worship experience. There is strength in group worship. Some people in sorrow say, "I don't believe I can go to church again." They go back home and to other places where they have known the presence of their beloved, but it takes extra courage for some to go back to church. Many find themselves strangely impelled to go, and they find strength in such an experience.

Then there are individuals who go to church to enjoy the fellowship with other worshipers. They need the human touch, the friendly voices in song and conversation; and they find relief from anxiety and loneliness. Still others need the worship experience for reidentification and reaffirmation that they are children of God.

The Church Family May Help

At times the person asks, "Can I trust my church to help me?" Others will say, "I want my church to be the last to know" or "I'd really prefer that my church not know about this." People may even join another church to avoid the gossip.

Love is the law of the church and the badge of discipleship. Brotherhood is a spiritual creation, as human fellowship is based upon a common fellowship with Christ. Church members need to be trained in the fine art of living together. The chief weakness of many churches is in their dwarfed affections and stunted sympathies. Superficial contacts often pass for fellowship in the church and people move on, lonely and anxious in their craving for supportive friendships. They pass to secular groups to find the kind of acceptance and intimate warmth they hear defined, but seldom implemented, in churches. The source of warmth in the church is human fellowship. When the church is such a loving fellowship, the single again may find an unusual amount of strength and help.

Sitting alone in the worship service may be a problem to you if you are accustomed to twosome worship. This can best be alleviated by sitting with friends until you make an adjustment. If you have children, sitting together as a family is even better. This kind of family or friend "togetherness" strengthens the sense of fellowship in worship.

What Churches Can Do

Church leaders should consult singles again about their needs, and serious attempts should be made to meet them. Church people often say about a grief-stricken person: "What she needs is to be kept busy." This may or may not be true. Maybe her readjustment problems are keeping her busy enough without having the added demands made by the church. The divorced person may *need* to be kept busy, only to have the church shy away from asking him/her to assume a place of responsibility. Why not talk with the singles again about their needs instead of assuming that the church leadership really knows and understands?

The church family often helps with adjustment to grief, but care should be given to provide this fellowship and ministry

112

for an extended time. Overdependency should be discouraged, but people in grief are often forgotten too quickly.

In economic adjustment, the church may save some from so-called "friendly advisors" who would cheat or defraud. Legal advice and money management counsel could be provided by church committees composed of members with expertise in these areas. Experienced retired people offer a wonderful resource for this service.

Church leadership should be aware of community resources such as health services, family counseling services, job training opportunities, and so forth. It is easy to make a list of such resources and have it available.

A Wide Variety of Possibilities

Many churches provide day-care services for children. For the single again opportunities for employment, recreation, study, and training often hinge on getting adequate care for the children. This is by far the most crucial service for many one-parent families.

Volunteer homemaking service or nursing corps could be made available for around-the-clock care in cases of emergencies, such as when children are ill or the parent is hospitalized. One church found a need for volunteers to assist a young person with physical therapy. Three persons were required each day to go to the home and do the work. The pastor, in making the appeal, said, "Few times is a church ever given a better missionary opportunity right in her own door than this."

Recreational programs and some very extensive recreational activities are offered by many churches. Special attention should be given so that children of one-parent families are not overlooked. Transportation and custodial care may be necessary. Summer camp funds could well be provided for some children. Would it be too much to ask that in some cases of disadvantaged parents funds be provided for the parents to attend conferences or retreats?

Fellow church members could provide holiday outings for parent and children or permit the parent to have recreation time off without the care of the children. Big Brother and Big Sister groups have been formed in some churches to provide certain professional counseling services for the children of one-parent homes.

Church family life education programs should include the singles again. Often they feel left out of everything at the church. Church library and curriculum materials are greatly needed. While many of their problems are similar to others, there are unique situations, some of which have been discussed.

In some areas, churches may need to help provide suitable housing for singles again. Few churches desire to go into the housing business as such, but often church leaders know where housing can be found at reasonable cost.

The church may sponsor a singles fellowship for the entire community—for fellowship, study, and ministry. It should not be a mere social club but a Christian fellowship where ideas and issues are explored through discussion, evaluation, and practical application. The organization pattern should be simple. Such a fellowship may well result in the members' rendering a better personal ministry through their respective churches and denominations.

Many churches are establishing a strong singles department in the Bible School and/or a singles fellowship on Sunday night. Churches may sponsor breakfasts on Sunday morning or a coffee hour. Some have a weeknight Bible study for this group. Alta Woods Baptist Church, Jackson, Mississippi, sponsors a "coffee talk" each Saturday night with an open house in the home of the Sunday School teacher. Many churches are now sponsoring annual retreats or seminars for the single-again group. Jackson's First Church sponsors both a retreat and a seminar such as outlined in the following sample program. The seminar is made available to all churches and denominations.

AN INVITATION TO THE SECOND

DIVORCE ADJUSTMENT SEMINAR

A Christian look at the open doors of hope
and adjustment for the divorced person.
5:30 - Fellowship   5:45 - Seminar, Fellowship Hall

OCTOBER 3 - "DIVORCED . . . and still an authentic person of promise?"
Dealing with self-identity following divorce. Dr. Ray Huff, Clinical Psychologist - The Pineda Clinic.

OCTOBER 10 - "I BELIEVE IN DIVORCE . . . sometimes!"
What is the scriptural teaching on divorce? Dr. Bob Shurden, Professor of Bible, Mississippi College.

OCTOBER 17 - "GOOD GRIEF . . . and other possibilities"
The positive emotional healing of grief and depression. Nancy Potts, Center for Counseling, Houston, Texas.

OCTOBER 24 - "HELP . . . I'm a Single Parent"
The double duty of the single parent. Marjorie Rowden, Vice-President of College Relations, William Carey College.

—A Special Session for Adolescent Children offering help to youth of divorced families. Dr. Mildred Crider, Professor of Adolescent Psychology, Mississippi College.

NOVEMBER 7 - "THIS HAS/HAS NOT WORKED FOR ME!"
A group sharing experience.

NOVEMBER 14 - "PUTTING HUMPTY DUMPTY TOGETHER AGAIN"
Healing the battle scars of divorce (bitterness, forgiveness, guilt) Dr. Mildred Crider, Professor of Adolescent Psychology, Mississippi College.

NOVEMBER 28 - ". . . 'TILL DEATH DO US PART'. . . unless the law decrees it!" Your divorce and the law. Judge Stokes Robertson, Mississippi Supreme Court.

DECEMBER 5 - "BUT I MISS THE WARMTH AND THE TOUCH WHICH I EXPERIENCED IN MARRIAGE!"
Dealing honestly and creatively with physiological problems. Dr. James Travis, Director of Pastoral Services, University Hospital.

DECEMBER 19 - "PASTOR . . . do you marry divorced persons?"
A fresh biblical approach to the possibility of remarriage. Dr. Clark Hensley, Mississippi Baptist Convention.

FIRST BAPTIST CHURCH

Downtown Jackson   Frank Pollard, Pastor
Phone 948–8780   David Roddy, Minister of Education

Qualified singles should be considered for leadership positions. One divorcée said, "Some people act as if you lose your capabilities when you lose your partner." Churches take some very strange positions on the question of using divorced persons in places of leadership. Failures are permitted in all other realms except a marriage. However, this sort of situation is becoming more rare. Unless or until there are flagrant moral delinquencies, most congregations are willing to trust another "redeemed sinner" to teach other "redeemed sinners" and "sinners who are not redeemed."

Churches exist to build up persons in the mood of faith, not of doubt; of hope, not of despair; of love, not of denunciation and fault-finding. No doubt God judges the church by the height of her ideals, the range of her sympathies, the reach of her aspirations, the depth of her convictions, and the graciousness of her disposition. All church members should be concerned about the dimensions of the soul of the church. She represents the winsome, wooing Jesus, who said, "Come unto me all ye that labour and are heavy laden, and I will give you rest" and "Whosoever will may come."

Your Pastor as a Resource

Clergymen are sought by people in trouble because they are considered men of mature judgment who care for persons and who understand their differences. They are thought to be men of prayer and are sometimes accepted as men of authority who know what to do. Others seek out a clergyman because he is, in their opinion, one who knows God.

Why People Fear Going to a Pastor

Some people *do* fear going to a pastor, particularly if they have marital problems and are facing a divorce or have been divorced. In other words, singles again often shun the pastor. They give several reasons for this:

116

1. They fear that he is too busy to be bothered and will not take time with them.

2. They fear that he will not try to understand, that he will not really accept them as they are, or perhaps that he has no basis for understanding.

3. They fear he will jump to conclusions and won't hear them out and consequently give wrong counsel.

4. They fear that he will be judgmental and may condemn and label them, adding to their feelings of insecurity

5. They fear that he will withdraw or withhold his love and that they may be shunted aside.

6. They fear that he will not keep confidences. They've heard him use pulpit illustrations about visits he has made and may wonder if their problems will be aired the following Sunday if they should confide in him.

7. They fear that he will be shocked if they tell the truth. Most ministers, however, have heard nearly everything there is to hear about interpersonal relationships.

8. They fear they couldn't face him later. They do not believe they can be open with him and be accepted by him.

9. They fear that he really does not care anyway, that he's too involved in the institutional aspects of the church.

The Pastor Usually Helps

More often than not, people in trouble will find help from their pastor. He may not be especially trained in counseling, but he has some resources that are useful: his own experiences with God in reconciliation, his general knowledge of people in situations, and the confidence of the person seeking help. If the pastor does have specialized training, all the better. A pastor who has none would do well to follow the pattern of the "reality therapy concept" proposed by Dr. William Glasser. Simply stated, it is to discover: (1) where we are now, (2) how we got this way, with not too much emphasis on the past, (3) what the responsible alternatives are, (4) what is right, (5) what is best. Several things could be right, but perhaps one is best.

The pastor's responsibility, therefore, is to respond with his whole being to the person before him and to accept this person with profound reverence. Here is one created in the image of God who has missed the mark in some way. The pastor is not to give hasty or partial judgments but to stand with him, accept and trust him, and believe in his potential. The pastor, too, will respect his silence and his privacy. He will encourage continuance in the story as it unfolds, using brief, helpful responses. He will not attempt too much in one counseling session. For him to make another appointment gives hope to the person and suggests that the pastor is interested and wants to help. He can always give some assurance that there will be a way out.

Other Pastor-helping Circumstances

Permit a few other observations concerning the pastor as a spiritual resource. The suggestions are made to pastors and friends with the hopeful thought that some will be reading this, looking for additional ways to help singles again.

Pastors have their unique ways of dealing with those in grief and in delayed grief. Many have written on this subject, and it has been dealt with briefly in a previous chapter. The pastor should provide some help for newly separated persons. Too often the church is concerned exclusively with getting the couple reconciled to the marriage rather than assisting them in adjusting to the reality of separation and divorce. For those who have already divorced, however, the church should offer assistance in necessary adjustments. Emotional support and practical counsel from the pastor may well be in order to assist these persons in coping with the many demands associated with achieving satisfactory adaptation to the role of the single again. This support should be given, if possible, to both persons involved. One man reported, "When we separated, the pastor and the church members rushed to the comfort of my wife. No one seemed to realize that I was hurting, too."

A pastor may show special concern by meeting with groups of singles who desire to discuss special problems such as men who are maintaining motherless homes, parents of preschool children or teenagers, and so on.

As a pastor counsels with a divorced person, he should be conversant with all aspects of the situation. Special emphasis should be placed upon the psychological and spiritual problems the single again faces. He may have to deal with economic concerns, needs and care of the children, and health hazards of the home, as well as his own attitude toward the person. Should eventual remarriage be considered, he must have a position on this.

Referrals May Be Made

Most pastors recognize their limitations. They may need to make referrals to a counseling psychologist, psychiatrist, physician, attorney, or mental health agency. Referral definitely should be made when the troubled person seems to have a very serious personality disorder, a definite psychotic personality, is mentally ill, or when children have severe emotional disturbances. If a person is severely depressed, referral to a physician should be made.

What should the pastor's attitude be when he finds that one of his members had gone to a neighboring pastor or clergyman of another denomination for help? This is sometimes done for one of the reasons we've already stated, but more often it is done because the member is embarrassed for his pastor to know about his situation and prefers going to one who does not know him. Rather than be disturbed by this, the pastor should rejoice that his friend is seeking help in a time of need. He should not try to pry information from his fellow pastor, for this should never be divulged without the consent of the member. When one is not concerned with hanging spiritual scalps from his belt, he always rejoices upon learning that some-one is being helped by another.

Other Resources

Group activities in which you or your family may participate have already been mentioned. These could enlarge your interests and may be better than personal therapy. These experiences will be less personal than dating someone individually and will probably provide relaxation and fun.

When the question "How do I get back into circulation?" was raised one divorcee answered by saying, *"Keep* in circulation through your work, through the church, through clubs, through volunteer work, and through visiting friends."

There are many singles clubs or sponsored activities for participation by singles. One of the best known is Parents Without Partners, Inc. This is a national and international organization that exists to study the problems of single parents and describes itself as a nonprofit, nonsectarian, educational organization devoted to the welfare and interest of single parents and their children. Its program and activities are carried on by the volunteer work of its members through programs, discussions, and social activities for both parents and their children. *Single Parent* magazine is an excellent aid to its members. For more information you may write to Parents Without Partners, Inc., 7910 Woodmont Avenue, Washington, D.C. 20014.

Adult education classes will be attractive to some. The family service association in your city or county may have suggestions for available group activities. Community organizations often sponsor supportive programs similar to those outlined as possibilities for churches.

Many state Sunday School organizations and family life ministry section groups sponsor retreats and seminars for single adults. Ridgecrest and Glorieta Baptist Conference Centers offer such programs at times during the year, traditionally on the Labor Day weekend.

11
Should You
Become a Helper?

'Tis the human touch in this world that counts,
The touch of your hand in mine,
Which means far more to the fainting heart
Than shelter and bread and wine;
For shelter is gone when the night is o'er
And bread lasts only a day,
But the touch of the hand and the sound of the voice
Sing on in the soul always.

Anonymous

Troubled people turn to someone they respect. This person has significance to them regardless of whether he is a bartender, a pastor, or a friend. Usually they turn to someone they like and one who by attitude or action has shown that he cares for persons as *persons*. Many people prefer that this listening person be one who has faith in God. There are three things the listener should refrain from saying: You shouldn't *feel* that way! You shouldn't *talk* that way! You shouldn't *act* that way! His primary task is simply to listen. He has what Dr. John Drakeford calls "the awesome power of the listening ear." The troubled person wants to talk, sometimes to ventilate, to simply talk out his frustrations, his fears. At other times he wants to talk in order to clarify his own attitudes and feelings. He may want to relieve his conscience, to make confession. He may talk to explore alternatives, to decide just what to do.

Suggestions for Active Listening

Perhaps it is your turn to listen. Here are some practical pointers:

1. Do your best to listen with your heart—or, as some say, with the third ear. Try to hear through what is being said and what is really being felt and meant. What is the real situation? You are not concerned with sordid details but are trying to learn the exact status of the circumstances.

2. Be as supportive as you can. Do not give advice such as, "If I were you, I would do thus and so."

3. Do not prattle piously. Don't use Scripture merely as a poultice for a sore heart.

4. Do not try to manipulate your friend through prayer.

5. You will respect silences as you listen. Some people cannot endure pauses in conversation; yet people in trouble need to tell their story in their own way, according to their own time pattern. Interruptions at a time of pause may distract, or you may be tempted to jump to a conclusion that is entirely erroneous.

6. You may need to explore alternatives with your friend or help him raise alternatives. You could say, "What have you thought of doing?" or "What do you think is the better way?" or "Have you considered this?" You may be in the position to help your friend determine his ability to carry out the alternative that he has decided upon, to help him be realistic. Sometimes people in trouble become dreamers and are not able to think in realistic terms. You may be able to help one accept responsibility for the consequences of the alternative that he chooses to follow.

7. You may be able to turn your friend toward other help, such as pastor, counselor, or physician.

8. You may sense some responsibility yourself in helping decide what is right. Yet there is a word of caution here. Since this involves a judgmental matter, you must be sure the choice is in the realm of moral absolutes subscribed to by the person being helped.

So, in the listening process you are helping the troubled person talk it out, think it through, and consider alternatives. You can help him see what he really faces, help him understand his responsibility at the moment, and help him decide how he can act responsibly to fulfill his needs without injuring someone else. You may assume that he desires to do what is right as he sees right and build upon whatever potential there is for good in his situation. To this end, a listening friend is indispensable.

Tomorrow—a New Time for New Beginnings

Seldom do we find ourselves able to fulfill all our fondest dreams. We begin with high aspirations and worthy goals; but somewhere along the way, either because of circumstances over which we have no control or because of the results of wrong decisions, we find ourselves falling short of the mark we have set. It is necessary to readjust, perhaps to settle for less momentarily or even permanently. In this readjustment period we may crack up or compromise our personal convictions. We may find ourselves living on a much lower economic, social, or spiritual level than we have hitherto experienced. Or we may reassess our opportunities, count our blessings, and determine to try again for fulfillment. After this is done, you may discover that life takes on a new dimension that far surpasses what you have experienced before in your own inner being as well as in your relationships with others.

Most of us have a lot more time left than we think. The *best* of your life may well be the *rest* of your life. It is a supreme joy to remember that for more than thirty years I have observed this to be true of many counselees who became my friends.

Hope

My expectations for tomorrow
Are far more than a denial of today.
This hope-shaped preoccupation with a new beginning
Gives deeper meanings to what I know about yesterday,
And scatters the dark thunderheads of loss
Hanging tenuously over this day
So that I can live tomorrow as the new time it is.[1]

123

Suggested Readings

Anders, Sarah Frances. *Woman Alone: Confident and Creative.* Nashville: Broadman Press, 1976.

Blanton, Smiley. *Now or Never.* Englewood Cliffs: Prentice-Hall, 1959.

Bohannan, Paul, ed. *Divorce and After.* New York: Doubleday, 1970.

Briggs, Dorothy Corkille. *Your Child's Self-Esteem.* New York: Doubleday, 1970.

Brister, C. W. *People Who Care.* Nashville: Broadman Press, 1967.

Buck, Peggy S. *I'm Divorced—Are You Listening, Lord?* Valley Forge: Judson Press, 1976.

Cardwell, Albert. *Life Alone.* Nashville: Convention Press, 1976.

Claypool, John. *Tracks of a Fellow Struggler.* Waco: Word Books, 1974.

Clinebell, Howard J., and Clinebell, Charlotte H. *The Intimate Marriage.* New York: Harper and Row, 1970.

Crook, Roger H. *An Open Book to the Christian Divorcée.* Nashville: Broadman Press, 1974.

Despert, J. Louise. *Children of Divorce.* New York: Doubleday, 1962.

Drakeford, John. *The Awesome Power of the Listening Ear.* Waco: Word Books, 1967.

Duvall, Evelyn Millis. *Handbook for Parents.* Nashville: Broadman Press, 1974.

Duvall, Evelyn Millis. *Parent and Teenager—Living and Loving*. Nashville: Broadman Press, 1976.

Edwards, Marie, and Hoover, Eleanor. *The Challenge of Being Single*. Englewood Cliffs: Prentice-Hall, 1974.

Emerson, James G. *Divorce, the Church, and Remarriage*. Philadelphia: Westminster Press, 1961.

Gardner, Richard. *The Boys and Girls' Book about Divorce*. New York: Bantam Books, 1971.

Glasser, William. *Reality Therapy*. New York: Harper and Row, 1965.

Gordon, Thomas. *Parent Effectiveness Training*. New York: Peter H. Wyden Inc., 1970.

Guernsey, Dennis. *Thoroughly Married*. Waco: Word Books, 1976.

Hensley, J. Clark. *Help for Single Parents and Those Who Love Them*. Jackson, Mississippi: Christian Action Commission, 1973.

Hudson, R. Lofton. *Persons in Crisis*. Nashville: Broadman Press, 1969.

Hudson, R. Lofton. *Till Divorce Do Us Part*. Nashville: Thomas Nelson, 1973.

Hollis, Mace, Anders. *Christian Freedom for Woman and Other Human Beings*. Nashville: Broadman Press, 1975.

Hollaway, Ida Nelle. *When All the Bridges Are Down*. Nashville: Broadman Press, 1975.

Jackson, Edgar N. *Telling a Child About Death*. New York: Hawthorn Books, 1965.

Krantzler, Mel. *Creative Divorce*. New York: M. Evans and Co., 1974.

Lawson, Linda. *Life as a Single Adult*. Nashville: Convention Press, 1975.

Lofas, J., and Roosevelt, Ruth. *Living in Step*. New York: Stein and Day, 1976.

Lyman, Howard B. *Single Again*. New York: David McKay Co., 1971.

Mace, David R. *Getting Ready for Marriage*. Nashville: Abingdon Press, 1972.

McMillen, S. I. *None of these Diseases*. Old Tappan: Fleming H. Revell, 1968.

Missildine, W. Hugh. *Your Inner Child of the Past*. New York: Simon and Schuster, 1963.

Nelson, Martha. *The Christian Woman in the Working World*. Nashville: Broadman Press, 1970.

Oates, Wayne. *The Bible in Pastoral Care*. Philadelphia: Westminster Press, 1953.

Oates, Wayne. *Pastoral Counseling in Social Problems*. Philadelphia: Westminster Press, 1966.

Oates, Wayne, and Lester, Andrew. *Pastoral Care in Crucial Human Situations*. Valley Forge: Judson Press, 1969.

Pate, Billie. *Touch Life*. Nashville: Broadman Press, 1974.

Pate, Billie, and Bowman, Norman. *New Beginnings*. Nashville: Broadman Press, 1976.

Payne, Dorothy. *Women Without Men*. Hyattsville, Maryland: Pilgrim Press, 1969.

Scanzoni, Letha, and Hardesty, Nancy. *All We're Meant to Be*. Waco: Word Books, 1974.

Schuller, Robert H. *Self Love*. New York: Hawthorn, 1969.

Shedd, Charlie W. *Promises to Peter*. Waco: Word Books, 1970.

Shedd, Charlie W. *The Stork Is Dead*. Waco: Word Books, 1968.

Small, Dwight Hervey. *The Right to Remarry*. Old Tappan: Fleming H. Revell, 1975.

Stewart, Suzanne. *Divorced*. Grand Rapids: Zondervan, 1974.

Stapleton, Jean, and Bright, Richard. *Equal Marriage*. Nashville: Abingdon Press, 1976.

Warlick, Harold. *Liberation from Guilt*. Nashville: Broadman Press, 1976.

Watts, Virginia. *The Single Parent*. Old Tappan: Fleming H. Revell, 1976.

Yates, Martha. *Coping—A Survival Manual for Women Alone*. Englewood Cliffs: Prentice-Hall, 1976.

Special Study Activities

Overall Aim: To lead Christian singles again in a recognition of their wholeness in Christ, their freedom to become and to help in sorting out and coping with the various problems faced by the group. To ascertain the climate of fellowship toward formerly marrieds in their own church—conditional acceptance, nonacceptance, or unconditional love. To lead Christian solos to discover ways of reaching others who need help.

Plan of Study: Enlist a leader who will select three to five other singles again to review this book and help determine a method of approach such as (1) Have someone review each chapter in a once-per-week session. Easiest, but least productive. (2) Set up an adjustment seminar around the topics. Ask someone to be resource person on each subject and have dialogue by questions and answers. More productive. (3) With an assigned leader, team-review the topics with input from other books, personal experience, and group sharing on an informal basis. Possibly more productive.

Special Seminars: You may desire to ask the pastor or some other "authority" to lead a seminar for two or three Sunday nights on *grief.* This would be good for the whole church. Other suggested subjects: How do you handle guilt? How do you build or restore self-esteem? How do you build self-esteem in children? Living in Step: stepparenting, stepchildren, stepbrothers and sisters. Note the divorce adjustment seminar topics from chapter 10.

Getting Ready: Order or ask your church librarian to order the following (from the Baptist Book Store unless otherwise indicated). Alternate plan: Ask each participant to contribute fifty cents per week to a book fund for the purchase of these and other books you would like to read.

Several copies of *Coping with Being Single Again* from your Baptist Book Store.

Marie Edwards' *The Challenge of Being Single,* from Parents Without Partners Inc., 7910 Woodmont Ave., Washington D.C. 20014, or through your book store.

Anders, *Woman Alone: Confident and Creative.*

Hudson, *Till Divorce Do Us Part.*

Small, *The Right to Remarry.*

J. Lofas and Ruth Roosevelt, *Living in Step,* Step Foundation Inc.

Pate and Bowman, *New Beginnings.*

Lawson, *Life as a Single Adult.*

Special Suggestions for Sessions

Session 1. So we are single again!

· Serve refreshments for fellowship, beginning thirty minutes ahead of program time. Room arrangement determined by size of group, but be as informal as possible. Circle or semicircle preferred. Leaders seated with the group. Ask group members how they feel as singles again. These questions are to be considered personally. Answers are shared only if there is a desire to do so.

1. List some disadvantages you feel in being single again rather than married.

2. List some advantages you feel as single instead of married.

3. What have you found to be the most difficult adjustment made so far?

4. On a scale of 1–10, where do you place yourself as to progress in your adjustment?

5. On a scale of 1–10, how do you feel your close friends and relatives would rate your adjustment?

6. On a scale of 1–10, how do you feel your church has accepted you in your singleness again?

Use the last three questions as discussion starters on group feeling. Try to chart the group feeling on chalkboard or make a graph on poster board.

Continue with the study, asking someone to read abbreviated case histories of Buddy, Mary, John, and Sally. Consider each individually and ask the group to fill in other details they suspect are true in each instance. The leader should be alert for close identification in order to properly empathize with and understand these persons. Be alert for hang-ups that may be revealed by projection of imagination into the sketches.

Indicate how the study discussions will proceed, and get input for further suggestions as to content and procedure. List the subjects named on chalkboard.

Session 2. Who are you? Sign in, please!

Suggested readings for what is said about *wholeness* and *acceptance:* Scanzoni and Hardesty, *All We're Meant to Be,* chapter 5, pp. 54–59, and chapter 7, "The Single Woman," pp. 145–168; Hollis, *Christian Freedom for Women and Other Human Beings,* chapter 6, "Myths about Men and Women," pp. 78 ff. In examining these statements at this time, look at wholeness and acceptance rather than what may be said or inferred about the feminist movement.

Questions for Discussion

1. Where did you get your name? commonly used family name? mother's choice? father's choice? that of another relative?

2. How are you known? How do you refer to yourself? With what identity do you feel most comfortable?

3. React to the paraphrase of the quote from *All We're Meant to Be,* chapter 2, page 3.

4. Discuss the response of Jesus to a single.

5. React to the sentence "Jesus had more pressures to marry, no doubt, than young people have today." (It was expected of all young men. Marriages were arranged by parents.) Did Mary and Joseph feel that Jesus was different? When did they really recognize this difference as to deviation from tradition? What about other relatives? peer groups?

6. If Clinebell and Clinebell's *The Intimate Marriage* is available, ask someone to define briefly the dimensions of intimacy the authors outline. Singles can develop most of these in relationships with friends. An exception would be that of sexual intercourse. In terms of our being "sexual beings," all interrelatedness is sexual.

7. What is the meaning of the phrase "to celebrate your humanity"?

8. Close with Sarah Frances Anders' poem "Who Am I?"

Session 3. Good Grief!

1. Perhaps it would be good to ask the pastor or some compassionate Christian leader who has personally suffered to discuss the cycles of grief.

2. A brief but careful review of *When All the Bridges Are Down* by Ida Nelle Hollaway would be appropriate as a part of this study. Give special attention to chapter 7 and the comments of Dr. Penrod on pp. 76, 78, 81, 85, 88.

3. Review the outline on God forgets, forgives, loves—so forgive yourself!

4. Get group reaction to closing part of the chapter "Coping with Certain Hazards."

5. Close with Ida Nelle Hollaway's poem "Dawn Encounter" at the conclusion of chapter 9.

Session 4. Alone and bored!

1. Discuss with the group the difference between loneliness, privacy, and solitude. (See section on "Boredom.")

2. React to the statement "The cure for loneliness is meaningful relationships with others."

3. What triggers loneliness with you? List responses of group.

4. List activities or coping devices of the group members.

"When I am lonely I _____."
"When I am bored I _____."

5. List the spiritual resources you have for coping with loneliness.

Session 5. "Sticks and stones may break my bones, but words _____!"

1. On a scale of 1–10 (from no stigma to heavy stigma), ask each to indicate personal feelings from reaction of friends, relatives, fellow church members.

2. Ask if someone would like to share comments from (1) the curious, (2) the condemners, (3) the concerned.

3. Get reactions to the listing of reasons for the stigma given by Dr. Travis.

4. List on poster board: (1) Destructive responses (a) (b) (c)
(2) Creative responses (a) (b) (c)

5. Have your children felt any stigma? How have you coped with this?

6. React to "perhaps maturity is the key factor." Whose maturity?

Session 6. Your Money and Your Health

1. Ask a doctor to discuss health issues. (20 minutes)

2. Ask a banker to discuss budget and credit. (20 minutes)

3. Questions and answers. (20 minutes)

Session 7. The Solo Parent

You may want to have several sessions on this study. One could center around the special problems of parents with preteens. Another with the parents of teens.

Resource books could include: Duvall, *Handbook for Parents;* Duvall, *Parent and Teenager—Living and Loving;* Dobson, *Dare to Discipline;* Grant, *Discipline in the Christian Home.*

In another session you could discuss "What Christian Parents Teach about Sex."

Resources: Howell, *Teaching about Sex—A Christian Approach;* Broadman Sex Education Series; Duvall, *Why Wait Till Marriage.*

A profitable series of study about the number 1 problem of parents with children: Building self-esteem!

Resources: Briggs, *Your Child's Self-esteem;* Dobson, *Hide or Seek;* Gordon, *Parent Effectiveness Training;* Schuller, *Self-love.*

Session 8. Coping with Sexual Tensions

1. Study sexuality in a biblical perspective. Check these points and Scriptures: Our sexual nature is a part of God's purpose (Gen. 1:27); our sexual nature is good (Gen. 1:31). Sexuality is basic to our human relatedness (a) as persons (1 Sam. 18:1–3), (b) in marriage Gen. 2:18–24; 1 Cor. 7:3–5.

To be sexual is not sinful, although human sinfulness may

be expressed in the misuse of sexual gifts as in incest, rape, sodomy, homosexuality, bestiality, and adultery.

Sex may be used for other self-centered purposes such as manipulating, blackmailing, controlling, rewarding, punishing: "Unless you do what I want, I will not be good to you" or "You do not love me."

Sexual sin is not the unpardonable sin (Eph. 2:3–10).

One's whole being, including sexuality, may be dedicated to God (Rom. 12:1–2).

2. Note the ways of coping suggested in this chapter.

3. Give attention to the difference between sexual attraction and lust.

4. Consider Dr. Mace's statement, "A Christian Ethic of Sexual Behavior," quoted in chapter 7.

5. Note conclusion of section in answer to the question, "What does the single again do about sex?"

Session 9. Should the Single Again Remarry?

1. Point out the estimate that 80 percent of divorced persons remarry—most within five years (*U.S. News & World Report,* 13 January 1975). Statistically, second marriages do better than first marriages. Could it be because when you are number 2 you try harder?

2. List some practical considerations in remarriage.

3. What of the value of premarital counseling for considering second marriages?

4. Consider the various views concerning the biblical basis of remarriage. React especially to statements in the chapter from Barclay, Hudson, Small, and Oates.

5. How does the group feel about "realized forgiveness" as being the Bible basis for remarriage of divorced persons?

6. If possible, have someone review some significant pointers from *Living in Step* with emphasis upon considerations of putting two families together. This perhaps should be a special session.

7. Another special session could examine other factors to be considered in remarriage.

For additional sessions, these books are recommended for study: Mace, *Getting Ready for Marriage;* Clinebell, *The Intimate Marriage* (communication); Stapleton-Bright, *Equal Marriage* (roles); Guernsey, *Thoroughly Married* (sexual communication).

Session 10. Resources and Helpers

1. Have different people point up: (1) resources within, (2) how the church may help, (3) the pastor as resource.

2. Discuss advantages and disadvantages of going to one's own pastor for help.

3. Discuss how formerly marrieds may be helpers to those who are singles again.

4. Discuss the purpose and value of active listening.

5. Have someone read to the group the last section, including the poem, "Tomorrow—a New Time for New Beginnings."

Notes

CHAPTER 1

1. Lynne Scott. Used by permission.

CHAPTER 2

1. Harry Hollis and others, *Christian Freedom for Women and Other Human Beings* (Nashville: Broadman Press, 1975), pp. 37–38. Used by permission.
2. By Sarah Frances Anders. From *The Student*, March 1978. © Copyright 1978, The Sunday School Board of the Southern Baptist Convention. All rights reserved. Used by permission.

CHAPTER 3

1. Ida Nelle Hollaway, *When All the Bridges Are Down* (Nashville: Broadman Press, 1975). Used by permission.

CHAPTER 4

1. Jason Towner, *Warm Reflections* (Nashville: Broadman Press, 1977), p. 60. Used by permission.
2. *Single Parent*, September 1974. Used by permission.
3. Peggy S. Buck, *I'm Divorced—Are You Listening, Lord?* (Valley Forge: Judson Press, 1976). Used by permission.

CHAPTER 6

1. S. I. McMillen, *None of These Diseases* (Old Tappan: Fleming H. Revell, 1968), p. 74. Used by permission.

2. Smiley Blanton, *Now or Never* (Englewood Cliffs: Prentice-Hall, 1959), pp. 25–26.

3. Alice Skelsey, *The Working Mother's Guide to Her Home, Her Family, and Herself* (New York: Random House, 1970), pp. 17–18. Used by permission.

CHAPTER 7

1. Sarah Frances Anders, *Woman Alone: Confident and Creative* (Nashville: Broadman Press, 1976), p. 31. Used by permission.

2. David Mace, *The Christian Response to the Sexual Revolution* (Nashville: Abingdon Press, 1970), p. 114. Used by permission.

3. Roger H. Crook, *Christian Family in Conflict* (Nashville: Broadman Press, 1970), p. 42. Used by permission.

CHAPTER 8

1. Billie Pate and Norman Bowman, *New Beginnings* (Nashville: Broadman Press, 1976), p. 49. Used by permission.

CHAPTER 9

1. William B. Barclay, *Ethics in a Permissive Society* (New York: Harper and Row, 1971), pp. 202–204. Used by permission.

2. Dwight Hervey Small, *The Right to Remarry* (Old Tappan: Fleming H. Revell, 1974), p. 175. Used by permission.

3. Lofton Hudson, *Persons in Crisis* (Nashville: Broadman Press, 1969), p. 43. Used by permission.

4. Wayne Oates, *Pastoral Counseling in Social Problems* (Philadelphia: Westminster Press, 1966), p. 107.

5. Ibid.

6. Lofton Hudson, *Till Divorce Do Us Part* (Nashville: Thomas Nelson, 1973), p. 56.

CHAPTER 11

1. Billie Pate and Norman Bowman, *New Beginnings* (Nashville: Broadman Press, 1976), p. 46. Used by permission.